Once Upon A Mission

A Coming of the Age Saga of An American Seminarian On Scholarship in Rome

By

Robert Taylor

Lovingly dedicated to Margaret Taylor, my wife.

Table of Contents

Keys To My Diary

"Life is a succession of lessons." – Ralph Waldow Emerson
"We do not remember days. We remember moments." – Cesare Pavese

Introduction

Mixology and Mission
A Christmas Quarrel between Pope Francis and his cardinals in 2021 over Francis Suggesting to Replace the "Djinn and Tunic" model of Trent with One of Charity and Proclamation.

Besides assuming his name, the present Pope has also adopted the commission given by Christ to St. Francis in the chapel of San Damiano," Francis, go repair my house which, as you see, has fallen into ruin." As a result, Francis urged his cardinals, the "princes of the church," to **take off their armor**, discard the trappings of their role, forgo worldly glitter, and embrace humility." (from NCR Dec. 23, 2021) He reminded them of the humility of Naaman, the Syrian warrior in the Old Testament who was willing to acknowledge that it was Yahweh who won him the battle, not strategy and that his suit of armor served several purposes, i.e. battlefield protection and to cover up his **leprosy.**

It was a poignant biblical argument from a pope who apparently subscribes to the sagacity of the American actress, Tallulah Bankhead, **"Fill what is empty, empty what is full, and scratch where it itches."** In his role as teacher and to save the cardinals from themselves, Francis followed this speech by giving each Curia member three books promoting renewal. Of course, the elephant in the room was a lesson garnered from Benedict XVI's resignation, namely - - "Either paint or get off the ladder"

The Church's mission (according to Balthasar the theologian)

The role of **the church in** the world **is not to be some alternative society** that is shut off and enclosed, a community or society preoccupied with its internal affairs, a "spiritual society of the perfect" that exists side by side with the secular order. The whole justification for her existence lies in her communicating to the rest of mankind the universally valid truths concerning God's liberating and redeeming work with fundamental openness which, in itself, is **the continuation of God's involvement in** Christ for the sake of **the world.** The church only needs such visible structure as is necessary to permit her message and genuineness to be proclaimed convincingly in the world! (<u>Engagement With God</u> by Hans Urs von Balthasar pg. 32)

Towards a More Inclusive Church

In a kind gesture, Pope John XXIII demonstrated his pastoral sensibilities by installing porta-potties and showers among St. Peter's colonnades for the homeless, a welcoming and fatherly gesture to his disadvantaged children. Francis, his successor and present pope, offered his own "gauchada" (gift) for the masses when he called for the **Synod** to announce to the world, "Friends, Romans, and all beloved of God, (Urbe et Orbi) I've come to lend you my ears." (And let me tell you, Pope Francis has very sizable ears, <u>Open to God Open to the World</u>). He embodies in so many ways the prayer of St. Francis, "Make me an instrument of Thy Peace" although sometimes peace is "hard fought." As an Argentine, I can see him including as part of his coat of arms an instrument made for dialogue, the humble and soulful Bandoneon, a squeezebox that can move in staccato caminata with other instruments (guitars and violins) to seamlessly lend a distinctive sound and gravitas, to a tango session, OR, since the bandoneon has no fixed chords, nor rigid keyboard holding it back, it can execute "el cruce" (dance step) and accommodate new partners like Astor Piazzolla, a modern tango master.

Francis has that same flexibility. He typically comes to interviews unscripted and arrives looking to find points of agreement **and** opportunities for discovery. He truly is an Everyman comfortable with himself and considerate so as not to tread on the "Taos" of his dance partners.

Why Read books?

Mastering the masters must not be our goal when we read but our starting point. A book is a cradle, not a tomb. **Physically** we are born **young** and die **old**!

Intellectually, because we inherit the past, therefore we are **born old** and must **try to die young** (from *The Intellectual Life*, by A.C. Sertillanges published 1920, pg.172)

My Format

"What good is a book without conversations and pictures?" Wondered Alice. (Alice in Wonderland) formerly entitled Alice Underground

All artists start out as amateurs. (Emerson)

On Priestly training

We play at Paste 'Til Qualified for Pearl

Then, drop the Paste and deem ourselves a fool

The Shapes though were similar

And our new Hands

Learned Gem- Tactics- Practicing Sands

(Dickinson)

We don't remember days, we remember episodes.

****

*In this book I will use bold prints and different fonts (newspaper and Wikipedia style) as guardrails for readers unfamiliar with theological and philosophical jargon or who come from other denominations

My Two Papal Heroes
Pope Francis expands on the legacy of Papa John XXlll
Update: CNA the Catholic News Agency

Jonathan Liedi, reporting from Vatican City, Nov.1, 2023/15:36 announced that **Pope Francis is calling for a "Paradigm Shift" in theology** that is needed to deal with the profound cultural transformations in today's world. Francis' "motu proprio" calls for **dialogue between different denominations,** different religions, and invites non-believers to the table. He envisions **a theology** that is fundamentally, **contextual, transdisciplinary, and pastoral,** emerging from the concrete situations into which all people, are seen ("Dasein" - the "lived moment"), a theology offering plumb lines for believers, and talking points for humanity in general. Wow! A surprising agenda even for a man who has already broken ground within his own fiefdom by allowing trans people to be baptized and to serve as godparents to the baptized and witnesses at marriages. Francis is also known to champion ecological concerns and advocate for regulations regarding the use of AI. All this is **to the chagrin** of many conservative American bishops. Excelsior, Papa for your vision, saintly courage, and faith!" You've proven Fellini's assertion time and time again- **"Visionaries are the true realists."** UPDATE - the recently published: "Dignitas Infinita" calls for new **guardrails for moral theology** i.e. by embracing contemporary science while honoring biblical principles vis-a-vis mankind under the rubric of the "image of God." Sadly, in the past, moral theology seemed overly obsessed with the pelvis area while underplaying everything north of the midriff. There's no such fixation in God's "'artist's proof" of the human body as far as I can tell, (apart from a few special interventions: one surgical in the case of Adam, one a hip adjustment for Jacob, one mobility for the paralytic, and finally the miraculous birth for Our Lord from the womb of Our Lady). Apparently, God is not made in the narrow mold of **moral theologians, thank God.**

Catholic News Agency, Vatican City, Nov. 21, 2024: "Pope Francis wants a church history free from ideologies."

*****

Once Upon a Mission

This book is a coming-of-age saga of an American Seminarian on scholarship in Rome.

Time Capsule cir.1967-1972

Searching for God Rails

Quest

Like old Mother Hubbard, well known for her quest,

I sailed me to Rome where the learning was best.

To the bone-ified Jesuit training

To complete my priestly formation

I arrived and adored the location (who wouldn't?)

Their haute cuisine surpassed expectation

But my quest was not feasting

I had come to learn priesting

Through a practicum for ordination

*****

Part I

Background

My Back Story

A Tip of my hat to Virgil

In Virgil's epic poem, which we were assigned to read and translate in high school, one finds the touching passage in which Aeneas, the future "Father of Rome" is fleeing the flames of Troy carrying on his back his aged father, Anchises, who is clutching the "Lares," i.e. statuary images of the Trojan household gods which were now just as homeless as these two refugees.

My story is also a "Rome Coming," but mine takes the form of a surprising and welcome escape from the boredom of seminary life in the late '60s, where we were insulated from both the happy chaos of hippiedom and not-so-happy problems of our contemporaries (the draft) to reflect on — "God knows what!"

I cringe to remember the many mornings when my fellow seminarians and I dragged ourselves bleary-eyed to the chapel to sing Gregorian Chant before mister rooster could sound his pitch-pipe and then we marched in silence to breakfast and class. Newspapers, of course, were off limits while we were sequestered and living "the dream." We spent our free time talking, playing sports, or boxed in by volumes of theology in rooms and study halls with Cassell's Latin dictionary in easy reach. Little did we know that this stained and dog-eared volume was destined to follow a lucky few, (the "cream of the crop") overseas to Rome and the Gregorian University, our future place of study where all the lectures and exams both written or spoken, were rendered in Latin.

So, as the Vietnam war dragged on, we, who were exempted from the draft as divinity students, were ordered instead to report to Rome

(Church Headquarters) to complete our "officers" training via a rigid and traditional curriculum at the GREG (a curriculum dating from the Middle Ages).

Staying connected while overseas

While in Rome, I maintained my sanity, by spreading my wings a bit by writing an original theological article which was finally published by NAC after censorship. I also grew some "pin feathers" (by learning Italian) to fly with others already serving the poor. Fluency provided two benefits 1) a full immersion practicum for this budding missionary and 2) an exodus from the bell jar of seminary life.

Around the holidays, I managed to mail some souvenirs, photos, and literary lanyards (locally sourced) to my family, just as I used to do with plastic lanyards woven during the closing days of vacation in the Catskills. Some of my classmates also sent trinkets home (relics and cameos mostly) to keep their loved ones in a state of breathless anticipation of our upcoming ordination in St. Peter's Basilica (and perhaps to ask for a little more travel money to flesh out their lavish European experience. After all, who knows what hidden spiritual treasures await a savvy seminarian on pilgrimage to the French Riviera!)

And so, in celebration of my life abroad as a twenty-year-old, I come to you, my literary and clergy family, "bearing gifts" i.e. lanyards of stories and lessons based on my travels. I hope that what I share will resonate with your own spiritual "Aeneid" and that my tchotchkes match some of those on your mantle next to your Latin dictionary, your mood rings, a set of wind-up chattering teeth, and those whoopee cushions from bygone days (which is a distinct possibility since, while history doesn't repeat itself, it has been known to hiccup.) And so, friends here's to sacred memories L'chaim! Without memory, your dog couldn't find his bowl, life would only be the current page on the calendar, melodies would dissolve into a cluster of disconnected notes, and your epitaph would be limited to R.I.P. From what exactly?---Too late to matter!

A challenge from Papa John XXIII who called Vatican II

Years before my scholarship to Rome, I heard this challenge from the visionary Pope, John XXIII, "We are not here to curate a museum. We are here to cultivate a garden." (A. G. Sertillanges would agree) I'm sure Papa John (Pizza be to him) had in mind Nietzche's disdain for so-called "Antiquarian History" that categorically embraces the past "like a tree content with its roots." My youthful reaction was, "Amen, Papa John! I see where you're going with this. You're merely trying to pry traditionalists away from their rear-view mirrors and point them to the windows. Now, looking back, I think Pope John's analogy overstated his case a bit. By pitting the archivists who store and catalog cultural treasures (roots) against the movers and shakers of today, the Pope glossed over the fact that both activities, be it conserving (museums) or cultivating (gardens) are future-oriented and essential - the museum does this, by preserving a record of cultural excellence, (which Nietzche approvingly labeled "Monumental History") providing inspiration and points of reference for future ventures while the garden not only maintain known plants and vegetables with proven benefits in nurseries but cultivate new variants and more resilient strains. A successful Church needs both: Scholars and "Plant" Managers (excuse the pun). Like Jack in the fairy tales, we find purpose in both the beanstalk and the ax (growth and pruning) as we move forward in history. We render to Caesar the things that belong to Caesar (status quo) but also claim tax deductions and exemptions for ourselves to afford the latest pair of Pro tennis shoes (status Pro). St. Mathew himself struck a balance in proclaiming the "Good News" (Matthew 13:52) when he writes, "The kingdom of heaven is like a householder who brings forth from his cellar things old and new." (All Hail, the once and future Church)

Balancing the two hemispheres of the brain

Since the age of seven, I loved serving at the Mass (Introibo ad altare Dei.) where I celebrated God as one of the joys of my youth. If memory serves me, I especially liked assisting at Requiem Masses (for which we were paid one dollar) and during the season of Holy Week when, we, altar boys enjoyed extra important duties to perform and more lines to memorize. In the wonderland of my youth, there was <u>no sacred/secular divide, only</u> fun/interests (truth be told). There was a seamless interplay among all areas of my life e.g. art galleries, hikes in the Catskills, working as a Sacristan, reading books on science, etc. It was like moving among interfacing mirrors reflecting similar stories starring me but with appropriate wardrobe changes. For example, on Saturday mornings I went from serving Mass in my cassock to returning home and changing into dungarees to work in my father's Victory garden. Saturday afternoons, I dutifully went to confession (spiritual awareness) pausing to replace the votive candles in their rack for the Immaculate Conception, then I bolted home to decode and enjoy Mr. Wizard's newest invention (a pre-Rube Goldberg gizmo designed to teach kids science). Science wasn't taught in many parochial schools, possibly because of the Galileo debuncle.

"Watch Mr. Wizard" was therefore the first of my many sorties outside the standard curriculum, driven by a need to sample these so-called "forbidden fruits" firsthand.

<u>The "Watch Mr. Wizard"</u> science show was made for and featured kids. The show would open with its host, Don Herbert working on a contraption in his kitchen, and a neighborhood kid would visit, see the experiment in process, and ask, "What are we learning about today, Mr. Wizard?" Mr. Wizard would answer, "Well, son/honey, today we'll study the three ways heat is transferred. By the end of the show, that kid and I could explain the contraption, thus making us feel like junior

scientists! (and a bit nerdy). If I were given the chance to be on the show back then, I'd have asked Mr. Wizard to teach me how to make non-stick votive candles to honor the Blessed Mother and save my fingers from bleeding when I tried to pry the half-burnt candles out from their cobalt blue receptacles. Eventually, I came to realize, like Emily D., that the brain is wider than the sky (E. Dickinson) with space enough to house galleries and gardens, church and science, wizards, you, and me to boot. (Truth's many faces)

Getting back to Pope John's argument – instead of proposing a hypothetical museum/garden dichotomy, I'd like to point out, Papa John, that I know of museums with a garden attached, like Villa D'este in Italy, and the gardens and statuary surrounding Schonbrunn palace in Austria, not to mention the Vatican Museum and the Vatican Gardens. Q.E.D. Your Holiness! The museum/garden combo celebrates Beauty in all its forms, satisfies both hemispheres of the brain, and gives evidence of God and man's potential for collaboration. Without God's contribution, a museum would be just an empty box, with no dinosaurs, no gems, no planetarium nor evidence of the godlike powers loaned to artists and scientists throughout the ages.

Once mankind had broken the covenant with God, God took back Paradise but agreed to lease the land east of Eden to us in the meantime, and keep us in the loop until Jesus came to reestablish order through His death, grace, and an offer of frequent sacramental rendezvous.

Was salvation part of God's original plan? Dun Scotus thinks so! Still, after the Fall, the whole world had no choice but to wait eons before it could finally exhale and announce a paradox at the Easter Vigil, "O happy sin of Adam that merited such a Savior." which defies logic and justice in favor of Divine mercy. (HESED).

Note: Hans Gadamer, a philosopher featured in the theory part of this book, is another example of a guy like me with a foot in several worlds, with one hand, (or foot) in his father's domain, who as both chemist and agnostic, pulled Hans towards the sciences while on the other hand/foot, Hans yielded to his guardians, a pair of pietist aunts who worked equally hard at fostered in the lad spiritual and humanistic sensibilities like a life-long love of poetry and respect for belief systems (faith).

Breaking News: museums are updating their messaging in light of climate change by revising the sign on the T-Rex Skeleton in the Museum of Natural History from "Don't touch the exhibit" to read instead, "Warning! You could be next." (Timely words that carry a bite!)

*****

Trent Model of Church

Djinn+ Tunic
Contained – exclusive
A gentleman's cocktail

Vatican II church model
Young, welcoming, open to the world, sharing the good news.

Signs of The Times
Context:
The work of the Vatican II (1962-65)

I grew up as a pre-Vatican II Roman Catholic. My first premonition of seismic ecclesiastical changes in the offing came from my reading the works of progressive theologians, like **Schillebeeckx,** (who bundled the seven sacraments under the title "Christ **the** Sacrament of Encounter'") and **Karl Rahner** whose articles touched on everything under the sun. Besides new ideas from various dogmatic theologians, the Bible itself was being subjected to scrutiny by Biblical scholars using secular tools such as comparative religious studies, textual and form criticism, and archaeological discoveries, etc. All of this prepared us as seminarians (insiders) for the whirlwind to come. These were truly **exciting times for curious intellectuals!** Meanwhile, **Catholics in the pews remained oblivious** to these low-pitched rumblings until they exploded in the form of the Vatican II documents, which caught them totally off guard. Vatican II proved to be both awesome and terrifying. It had enlisted **the talents of major theologians of every stripe** and its results received overwhelming acceptance and approval by the majority of participants at the council (according to Bishop Barron on YouTube). But once the results were published, the Holy Spirit flew back to heaven, to offer IT and leave the church to work out the details and manage the blow-back. In her wake, the coterie of conservative theologians felt they had been stretched to the max and wanted to rest. Their episcopal counterparts who were dragged half-consciously through one Latin session after another led by classically trained scholars, started to realize the magnitude and implications of what they had endorsed. Evidently, when Pope John proposed the council, he not only cracked a window, he opened up a chute intended to shuttle traditional clergy onto the conveyor belt called NOW. (c.f Bishop Barron YouTube on Vatican II).

On the sunny side of change, the more avant-garde members of the council were energized and ready to "push for Vatican III," To them, I shout, "Excelsior, adventurers! Let the new day dawn. Throw your cares aside!" As Nietzche observed, "**There is always some madness in love. But there is always some reason in madness**."

Soon the swagger of pre-Vatican II Catholicism, which considered itself the **only authentic Church** of Jesus Christ, (the infamous, "The Boast of Best Worlds" Syndrome) assumed a **more ecumenical tone, thank God,** with cosmic implications. As we know many dramatic changes in history begin gradually, stealing **in on padded feet.** Take, for instance, the clandestine swapping of the original formula of Coca-Cola with a saccharin variant which betrayed one's palate and insulted the booze. Or another example: remember how those delicious wax paper-wrapped Devil Dogs of my day were replaced without warning by insipid knock-offs whose only virtue was their longer shelf-life? OR, how about those sturdy whalebone corsets of yesteryear (capable of breaking the toes of a misanthrope like W.C. Fields)? They were suddenly exchanged for the flimsy tummy trainers of today. What clandestine gears produced such mischief? Who can say? But this much is certain - the Vatican II left liberals surfing the breakers while the die-hards paddled desperately in the shallows.

Reactions to Vat II

1. The oddest **negative** reaction to these **top-down** proclamations from the council fathers (aka crows in the crow's nest), came from folks who wanted to dig in and hold their ground by bringing back the **Latin Mass**. Most of them didn't speak Latin (a dead language). The priests who offered those Latin Masses and prayed the Breviary weren't fluent in Latin (nor was I when I entered the Greg). Christ didn't speak Latin at all and I suspect that in heaven, Latin Masses on earth give Jesus a case of the "willies" (flashbacks) upon hearing on the lips of the celebrant the

same language used by the soldiers who cursed Him on the cross, "O tempora, O mores!" O well, Mazel tov, Yeshua! I suspect that even today, Jesus might find a performance of <u>Carmina Burana</u> a wee bit "Orff-putting," linguistically speaking. Jesus is definitely not a Lain lover.

2. **Positive** reaction- On **the liberal side of the street,** the changes were welcomed and **overdue**, so understandably, **some people overdid them**. Nuns who had previously been forced to shuffle around in Medieval costumes, i.e. habits, corrugated with hundreds of pleats that needed daily ironing, and antique shoes that just looked old, (no matter how often you polished them or what young ankles displayed them). Yes, these long-suffering nuns shouted, "Thank God! Now we look somewhat NORMAL, maybe **stylish** even!"

Of course, **some ugliness** also surfaced in the process. A few convents in Queens, N.Y. actually built walls in their nunneries to separate the living quarters of the younger nuns from those stick-in-the-mud minions of their Mother Foundress. Some of them labeled these changes as "an experiment in smaller communities." But that didn't fool the postman who now had to deliver packages to opposite ends of the convent.

Enterprising nuns tirelessly "manned" the sewing machines, creating the latest in religious apparel for themselves, and also designed colorful felt banners that displayed classic biblical sayings such as, "Knock and it shall be opened," which only invited scoundrels like me to inquire, "How late do you stay open, Sister?"

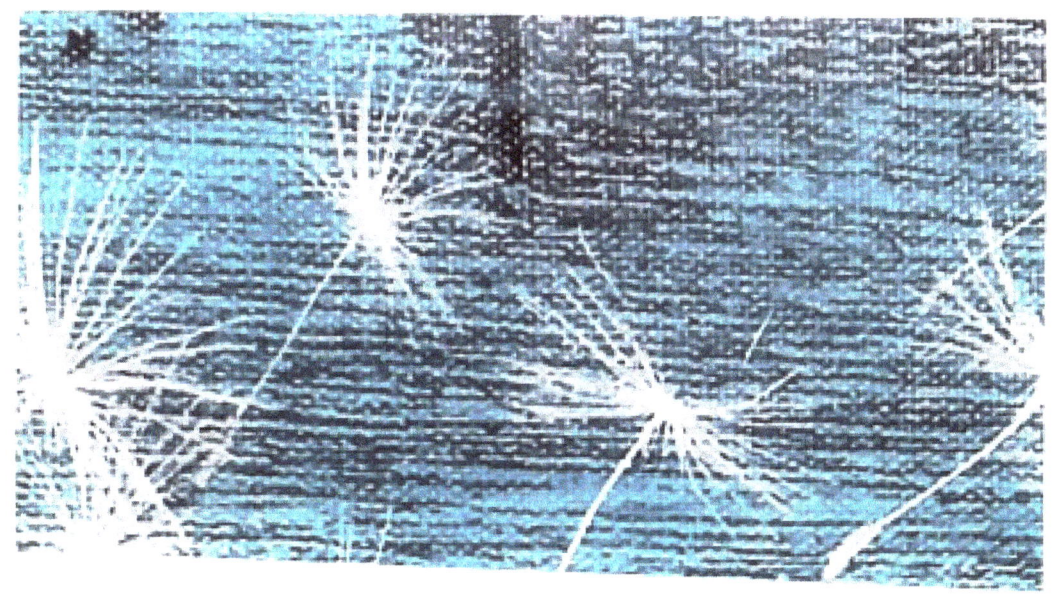

My take on these excesses and short-lived Rumspringas is simply this: the Catholic Church, as a top-heavy institution, had produced a flock of co-dependent sycophants for centuries, willing to "pay, pray, and obey" without question. Truth be told, Mother Church had neglected to **"piety-train"** her offspring in the basics of "SPIRITUAL SELF-CARE!" (preferring instead to enroll them in authorized **daycares** like Opus Dei and sodalities or a **military school**, like the Swiss Guard and the Knights of Columbus, or assign them guardian ad litem i.e. picking **a patron saint** at baptism). History should have prepared her for a day of reckoning, empires collapse and children grow up. Mother Church shouldn't have been so surprised to eventually hear a few members grumble and say, "We're not children anymore. We deserve some respect. We're professors and doctors and parents ourselves. This is not the Middle Ages. WE CAN READ!" Pardonnez-moi ce caprice d'enfant, Pape Francois. I'm only proffering a few "bon mots" to advocate, as you do, for a more critical, mission-minded, and democratic church.

In contrast, the Episcopalians in Colonial America had no choice but to become spiritually self-reliant **by arriving** in this country decades before **the clergy**. As a result, the laity of these churches became more inclined to debate issues and update polity as the needs arose (Parliamentary style) and partner with clergy when they finally arrived.

Sadly, the waves of the Vatican II hit the traditional RC laypersons like a tsunami. Just imagine their shock on reading Yves Congar, declare in Vat II that **Baptism, not Holy Orders**, (priesthood) was the **primary sacrament of mission**, thereby, giving laypersons seat and voice at the conference table of evangelization (also c.f. Pope Francis on Synods). Who then are <u>missionaries</u>? **Answer: All the baptized!** (reminiscent of Luther's teaching about the <u>priesthood</u> of **all** believers. Na?)

<u>What would my mother say about this?</u> Bless her heart (having labored and sacrificed for years to make me <u>someone Special</u>, namely, **a Roman Catholic Priest**) **"Rhinestones for diamonds,"** that's what she'd said. **As for my dad, who before passing away, used to tell his cronies** with a brogue and a brag, **"We gave him to God; so, the hell with him."** To both, I say, **"Sorry, you guys.** I eventually **did** what you wanted me to, **albeit by joining a slightly** different team. **I just couldn't wait for Pope Francis' Coronation to suit up again and take my clergy shirt out of mothballs.**

****

Media Breakthrough
Catholic TV Evangelism in the US <u>before</u> Vat-II

In the 50s, Bishop Fulton J. Sheen made a breakthrough in adult religious education by producing a TV show called, **"Life Is Worth Living,"** which became so popular that it stole the audience from The Milton Berle Comedy Hour, the number one offering at that time. Sheen's sense of humor, theatrics, antagonism to psychiatry and communism, and his advocacy of family values <u>touched a cultural sweet spot</u> in this largely Protestant country. Even children loved "Bisshy Sheen!" My whole family loved Bishop Sheen. I loved his genius and style. When he told troubled souls, **"Get off your couches and get down on your knees."** America applauded.

He had the smile of a leprechaun and an Irish immigrant's love of country and he'd often opened his show with a grin and a joke like, **"Today's show is entitled "The Ages of Man which are threefold: youth, middle-age, and my, you're looking good!"** Sheen ended his show by lifting his hands and saying, **"Good night and God <u>love</u> you."** **which is of course less ominous than saying, "Good night and Lord <u>help</u> You.**

Catholic Evangelism Today in the USA

His successor today, a conservative, Bishop Robert Barron, can't count on receiving the same welcome and adulation as his predecessor in our divided and secularized America. Seen as a cultural anachronism, Bishop Barron, nevertheless boldly mounts a well-funded and staffed pulpit with his own genial smile and winning demeanor, but with a more belligerent undertone than his predecessor as he battles opponents past and present in defense of the faith. He is philosophically adept and orthodox, but today's world is not as simple, respectful, or curious about Catholics as it was back in the 50s. Not even Catholics are! It's time to stop winding the sundials.

Nevertheless,

Bishop Barron is the model of a modern church apologist,

With tales of hagiography to entertain the rest of us.

He knows midrash and targums just as well as any rabbi might.

And discounts the fundamentalists, and there I think he might be right).

And when it comes to figures of religious opposition,

He can dissect Marx's and Feuerbach's with surgical precision.

Still, solutions formulated for other time's requirements

May miss the mark for folks today who cannot see their relevance.

(ME)

Barron's presentation of traditional teaching is laudatory I admit, but I would prefer him to be less dismissive of non-Catholic positions (shades of late-stage Cardinal Ratzinger) and more like **Pope Francis, who champions dialogue over proselytizing** (and <u>**HE'S THE Pope**</u>!) Francis eschews exceptionalism (c.f. Francis' book entitled, "Open to God. Open to the World") and calls for diffident theological renewal, quoting the protestant theologian Paul Tillich's **criticism of evangelization today** as an **attempt to answer questions that no one is asking. My class of 1967 anticipated, to some degree, the future agenda of Pope Francis' reforms at least regarding priestly training.**

Interestingly, when Tillich opted to correlate the questions of the day with insights rooted in the Bible, surprisingly, he hardly had any **biblical citations** in his three-volume work called <u>Systematic Theology</u>. Shocking or egalitarian? Your call.

I think Bishop Barron would do well to rein in his zeal, holster his weapon, and take the high road as Pope Francis and Bishop Sheen modeled. While Sheen was willing and ready to **contest** ideologies, he drew the line at criticizing his chief rival, the comedian **Milton Berle,** who was known to do <u>skits in drag</u>. Then again, how could Sheen **point the finger** at poor old Uncle Milty when Sheen himself appeared on camera wearing a cassock (dress), a flowing cape (flummery), and a pectoral cross (cross-dressing?) Be that as it may, "**Love ya, 'Bissy Sheen!'"**

In these pages I wrestle with two questions: 1) How will our faith claims survive the barrage of contradictory positions and the challenges of a changing and multicultural planet and 2) How to encourage our contemporaries to notice and heed the experiential markers of God in the world which invite a spiritual response, e.g. the transcendental qualities, of goodness, truth, and especially, beauty. (To see God's beauty tangible and comely in His masterworks).

Should Songbirds Be Caged?

I'd rather learn to sing from a single bird then to teach ten thousand stars not to dance.
E. E. Commings

My Seminary days in the United States
Before my call to Rome (1958-1966)
My Perch and Pedigree

In the summer of 1967, before the fall semester, six vacationing seminarians were put on **notice** that they weren't going to return to their studies in Long Island. Instead, the Diocese of **Brooklyn, NY was sending them to Rome** on a **full scholarship** for four years to be trained at the prestigious Pontifical Gregorian University, better known as the Greg, which was the alma mater of popes, prelates, and scholars for centuries. Never before had my diocese chosen to **send so many** students there for advanced studies as in 1967. I, being one of them, was, of course, both surprised and relieved to hear their decision. Had my dad lived to see this day, as a New York City cop, would have had to be restrained from convulsing with joy at the news. If you're **lucky** enough **to be Irish**, having both a priest and a policeman in the family was like owning a leprechaun's pot of gold. **My father had championed my vocation from altar boy to seminarian** before he passed away. My father was a generation older than my mother. He was a guy from another century who sang Vaudeville ditties like "Way down south in Elizabeth New Jersey. There was a girl whose name was 'dirty neck.' She was the pride of the Lackawanna Ferry. And when she cried, the tears rolled down her back." **or** this gem, "In the middle of July, in the coldest kind of weather, when it's too cold for two to sleep alone, then one must sleep together." He also liked the **1921 hit song** "Peggy O'Neil" which contains a line that describes me as a youth to a T, **"Sweet personality, full of rascality, that's MJPD (my initials back then)."** Today, to be honest, I'm presently on the semi-sweet side of the spectrum, but with <u>more</u> flavonoids than ever before.

My dad wrote two poems that I know, one **for** a pair of **nuns in** celebration of their golden jubilee and **the other** inspired by a magazine cover depicting a boy nursing his sick dog. The dog caught bronchitis from rescuing a little girl's doll from a pond. This poem was published.

Two of my dad's uncles were priests, Fr. John Downing, honored and remembered fondly as the pastor of St. Francis Church. The people named him "The Pope of Providence R.I." and Fr. Mortimer, his brother, who had **conflicts with his bishop** like I had and wrote poetry (also like me). He **built a chapel** at Hyannis Massachusetts. in1915. Both represent the "academic" limb of my family tree.

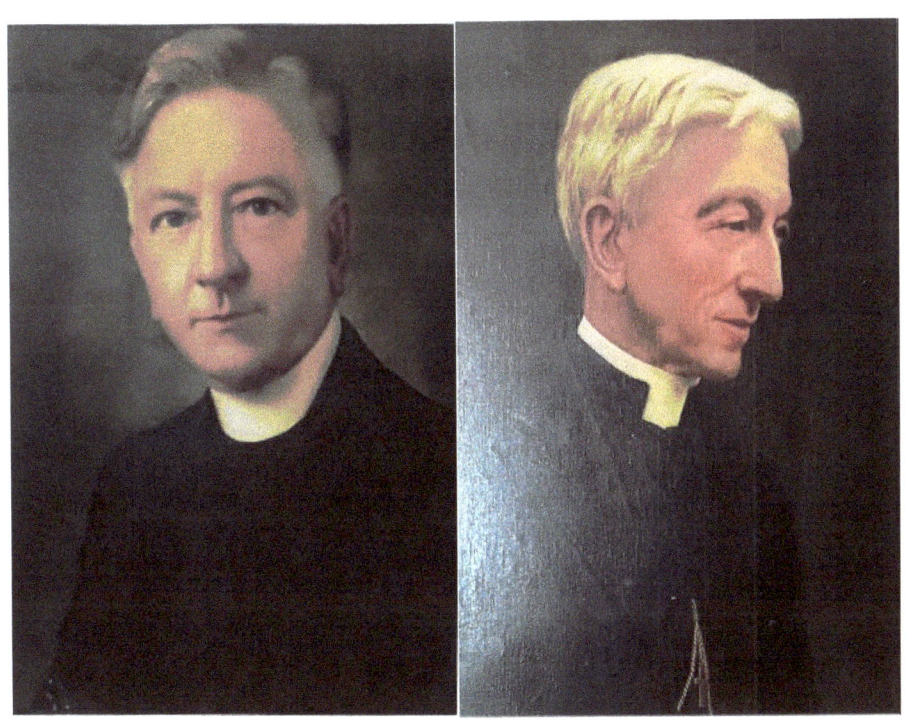

My mother, a child of immigrants from Italy and Austria, and top of her class in High School had always considered me special as her firstborn. Her side of the family included **two famous musicians** and craftsmen. (Her father was the tech designer for the **Panavision projectors** that debuted the film, "White Christmas") Her hopes for me were fueled by my parochial school teachers, nuns of the **Order of the Sisters of Mercy** (but don't let the label fool you. They were strict) They swore on their girdle of rosary beads (prayers from the hip) that my class was the most gifted they had seen in a decade and they **labeled me, "Mr. I.Q."** Mom was sure I'd become a Pope. It broke her heart and mine when it turned out that **after 3 years of ministry**, the **I.Q. stood for 'I Quit.'** "Diamond for rhinestones. Diamond for rhinestones," she moaned. Bless her heart.

I had entered the **seminary** system **after 8th grade** with a fist full of scholarships, one of which was called the Pope Scholarship which I naturally assumed was recognition from the Vatican itself. But, alas, I found out that it was only the **Alexander Pope scholarship.** Alexander Pope was a satirist known as the **'Wasp of Twickenham'** and was in no way a pretender for the papal throne. **Sorry, mom, wrong pope.**

A cautionary tale

After six years of successfully maintaining high grades and a low profile in Brooklyn, **I became** more **assertive** and **visible** in a **major seminary** on Long Island, probably causing my sainted father a postmortem coronary in the land over the rainbows. I can imagine him shouting, "D—n it, Laddie! You're going to get yourself kicked out like your brother Ray did!"

Seminary Casualties

Yes, **my brother Ray** was asked to leave the High School seminary for raising provocative questions. With no bad intentions on his part, he asked the religion prof why Jesus gave stigmata to saints in their hands when we know the Romans nailed the crucified through the wrist. "Where did you get that stuff?" the prof bellowed, "From Jehovah's Witnesses? Why can't you be like your big brother?" Truth be told, I put that bee in my brother's bonnet. But, God's providence is hard to fathom, He chose to make my disgraced brother a millionaire and me, "The chosen one," as poor as the Cure of Ars. Although, personally, I would have preferred He'd have made my brother Ray, half a millionaire and me a scholar with rich patrons.

After being expelled, my brother Ray went on to earn a B.A. in art from St. John's University. Afterward, he rented a studio in Manhattan and eventually **won an Emmy** for producing the documentary, "Stealing Lincoln's Body" on the History Channel. That was followed by another documentary on the visage of the man depicted on the Shroud of Turin entitled, you guessed it, **"The Real Face of Jesus."** He earned his pot of gold. But be warned. Don't ask my brother about the nail prints on the Shroud or you may need a shroud yourself. **PTSD** can be ugly! (**Post Traumatic Shroud disorder**).

We children owe a lot to our father for gathering his brood around the patriarchal bed each night to recite the rosary and listen to stories of Fatima, Don Bosco, The Little World of Don Camillo, and a satirical anti-Protestant epic poem called, "Patty Blake Sojourn Among the Soupers," which described how those "Black Protestants" tried to bribe Irish Catholics away from the faith with soup during the Great Famine. Quite a legacy.

From noticing to projecting to profiling and out the door

Four years after they expelled my brother Ray for being curious, **the faculty expelled my bro, brother C, for being calm. He was the only African-American candidate in the place,** a gifted organist who generously played the organ for us during daily services. He had a broad

27

smile that could be interpreted as a smirk by authority figures if so inclined. Plus, mischief and talent allowed him to play hymns on the manual while simultaneously tapping "Take me out to the ball game" on the pedals. The faculty never caught on but we did. What Brother C did was nothing new. In the 1500s when the council of Trent forbade using secular music in church services, the composer Frescobaldi circumvented the edit by introducing in the liturgy 'canzones' which mimicked the popular songs of the day but went undetected by the clergy who never listened to the pop charts latest hits. . When the faculty decided to give Brother C a boot, they invoked a process called discernment which they stole from the Jesuits. **DISCERNMENT**? Since when is racial prejudice synonymous with discernment? What they really found so offensive was **his attitude**. As a black man, they felt he should have been angry, but he wasn't. Just <u>too</u> **bougie** for his good, they opined him with his upper-class organ lessons and vacations in Martha's Vineyard. They presumed that there must be some hidden rage lurking below that black skin and so, "He had to go!" Thanks to their reptilian brain and prejudice, they lost, in my opinion, an excellent priest.

<u>Speaking of our Brother C:</u>

I recently read how the famous theologian Hans Urs von Baltasar, an accomplished musician, chose **organ-playing** as a metaphor for Jesus's earthly sojourn during which the Lord improvised themes of truth and love on the **keys** (virtuosity) while simultaneously tapping out a perpetual continuum to the Father **on the pedals** (as an obedient SON). My friend, Brother C, our ousted Pied Piper, will be remembered for both <u>treating his buddies in the bleachers</u> to "popcorn and cracker jacks" between innings (fellowship) while delivering an inspiring performance for all present. Thank you, Brother C, for your pastoral sensibilities and talents!

I was hurt, outraged, and frightened by these two losses and **tried to analyze them**. If my brother's tragic flaw was curiosity, and my friend's was self-confidence, what would they find objectionable in me? Well, they wouldn't have to look too far. I handed them one on a silver plate when I discovered philosophy. It was love at first cite (ibid). I was swept along in its riptide like St Augustine was after reading Cicero's "Hortensius." Of course, <u>our</u> **philosophy** courses couldn't compare with what thundered and merited debating in the aulas of secular universities. No, ours was **fun-sized**, an example of the only brand of philosophy judged to be Catholic-friendly by Leo XIII and Pius X, - **Thomism**, (but with a Kantian twist). Ah yes, St. Thomas, to you we forever raise a glass and sing, "There's no 'ism' like Thomism, like no 'ism' I know." Funny, though, our professors never explained why Thomas **went silent** after writing his Summas. Were those writings superseded by a mystical experience, thereby calling their worth into question? Maybe! Thomas himself did mention the 'via negativa' a time or two in his writings **which claims we know more what God <u>is not</u> than what <u>He is</u>**. Our analogies <u>can't</u> match his excellence.

*****

Academics

Philosophy

Philosophy with Fr. Smith (1966)

My college philosophy professor in the major seminary in Huntington, Long Island, was Fr. Smith, a dead ringer for comedian **Stephen Colbert**. He used to sit behind his desk and translate from a French cahier or notebook written by **Joseph Maréchal**, a Louvaine Professor and a key figure in the movement called Transcendental Thomism, which was Thomism in dialogue with modern thinkers like

Immanuel Kant. Kant caused a revolution in philosophy, a Copernican shift from the known to the knower, **from** the **objects** under investigation **to the structures of the knowing subject**-the **mind-field** called introspection.

Philosophical gears had to be shifted by Catholic thinkers such as **Maréchal** and he was up to the task. While Fr. Smith read us the notes of his master, he would customarily pause, formulate a question to move the narrative forward, then, lick his finger and turn the page. One could see him savor every lick as if it were buttercream on a Belgian waffle (Louvaine is in Belgium). I was mesmerized by this "love of wisdom" class. It was like science without the claptrap of instruments and measurements, something you could do in your head – science lite if you will. I was caught in the undertow and started raising my hand unprompted and "mirabile dictu" (holy smokes). **I started anticipating** the content of **the next page** before it was licked and turned. In other words, I actually outran the text of Marechal, a groundbreaking philosopher-theologian! I found out much later that Marechal also had a doctorate in both the **hard science**s (Biology) and **soft science** (Philosophy). He was a fully **bi-cameral man** whose ivory tower housed tools for all of his advocations: books, microscopes, net, specimen jars, etc. **Take that, empiricists**! This Marechal was **no one-act pony.** (By the way, there are many other examples of priests/scientists throughout history e.g. Johann Gregor Mendel). As a scientist, Marechal could deftly analyze **a murmuration** of crows scientifically then switch to the other hemisphere of his brain and respond to the same phenomenon aesthetically and theologically as wonders of God's creation (cf. painting of crows in a cornfield attached). I grant you, telescopes bring us new insights and closer to some secrets of the cosmos (hard science) but it's still nice to enjoy **the face** of the "**man in the moon**" on a starry night with an arm around your lab assistant. **(Oh, so soft** a science!)

In philosophy, I was introduced to dangerous new ideas like the Cartesian "method of doubt" – a real eye-opener for someone born into a Church where **doubt** was considered the **Petri dish of heresy.** Imagine getting permission to further one's knowledge by asking probing questions (such as, "What can I know for certain? Is there an external world? etc.), then breaking these conundrums into solvable subsets and axioms by using your experience and introspection as instruments. Fantastic! Once I tried it on for size, **in the words of James Brown, "I felt good, yada, yada, yada, ya."** In the blink of an eye, I morphed from a learner to a thinker and felt such a dopamine rush of ideas and discovery that one day I brazenly brought grapes to class and popped one in my mouth as pearls of wisdom left my lips (very playful but not so wise). Luckily, I caught myself in time by remembering how the hubris (perceived or imagined) of my brother and friend ended their priestly dreams. So, I prudently gave my professor back the spotlight and repurposed my energies toward packing my bags and changing my mailing address **from the Via Media of Aristotle to the Via Appia in Rome.** It was time to **get out of Dodge!**

Footnote: **Karl Rahner**, a theological superstar, whom I'll introduce later, was very taken by **Marechal's** interpretation of **St. Thomas' theory of knowledge** and used it as his point of departure for his 1936 dissertation on St. Thomas at the University at Freiburg. Marechal allowed Rahner to encounter St. Thomas in a more personal way, allowing Rahner to develop both his transcendental theology and philosophy (cf. the Mystical Way Intro p. xxxiv). Rahner was also fascinated by Marechal's study of **mysticism.** (cf. Rahner's book on the Mystical Way p. xxvi of the introduction). Rahner claims that embracing **Mysticism may prevent the Church from becoming irrelevant** and disappearing. (A question raised by Jesus himself, "When the Son of Man returns, will he find faith on the earth?")

****

Character Formation
The celibacy conspiracy - "Unblemished Lambs"

The life of celibacy demanded extraordinary safeguards to protect seminarians from "designing women." That's why our day-school seminary in the States designated Thursday as our day off and made Saturday a school day **to prevent us from mingling with our peers. As a result, we had an unrestricted run of empty basketball and handball courts in Brooklyn and Queens, less the pageantry of crowds and cheerleaders.**

Our faculty in the States outlawed certain "high risk" summer jobs such as lifeguards, bouncers, bartenders, and croupiers, leaving only gardening, stock boy, and paperboy as possible cash cows (Did you know Pope Francis was a bouncer before going to the seminary? Watch out, cardinals!). Even our families connived to ensure our social isolation. We were also obliged to get a spiritual report card from our pastors during summer break showing we attended mass **every** Sunday.

When I was eighteen, my sister disguised herself as a date and came calling to our house in Flatbush to invite me out. My mother answered the door and when she heard this hussy's untoward intentions, **Mom righteously slammed the door** in my sister's face, never recognizing that the caller was none other than Margie, her daughter, and my sister! Hooray! My vocation was protected and my sister was reprimanded for skulduggery. Still, I wonder whether my sister would have enjoyed the same degree of parental solicitude if she were in training to become a nun. Nah. Don't be ridiculous, friends! In those days, the vocation to the priesthood trumped lay brothers and nuns every time. For me, celibacy was basically a crypto form of sin-indoctrination that elevated abstinence beyond the peel and appeal of wedding bells. Unfortunately, I bought into their propaganda – bell, Book, and censor

Warning! You may detect **residual misogynistic overtones** and generalizations in my upcoming vignettes. Please chalk them up to verisimilitude. That is where I found myself emotionally at age 22, after living in a cloistered, all-male environment for years. Had I been afforded opportunities to have everyday contact with peers of both sexes, I might not have remained so clueless, immature, and chauvinistic.

*****

Brainwashing?
Company Men

In my experience and through informal chats with other Sems, I came to realize that our seminary training closely resembled the practices of another esteemed institution, the Spanish Riding School in Vienna.

With our superiors holding whips and lead-lines needed to put us through our paces i.e. to jump time-tested hurdles gracefully and in sync. OK! But here's the rub, what would happen if the horse had other plans? You can ask my brother how that turned out! To be fair, we were never "Oliver Twisted" into shape by extreme measures. Yes, we were indoctrinated but we were never drilled to the breaking point in the style of a master sergeant nor slapped into Satori by a zealous Zen Master (although, I have heard that after ordination some classmates voluntarily agreed to enroll in boot camp to become army chaplains while others submitted to gurus to become enlightened retreat masters) To them, I say, "De gustibus non est disputandum," which means, "If it's your thing, do what you got to do." Nevertheless, **seminary faculties** in the 60s **were in general** an autocratic and traditional cadre. Since **obedience** always implies and requires overlords, it is a **virtue imposed**. Play along and you may even get to hold the whip yourself someday. Frankly, becoming a bishop (overseer) or an equestrian trainer was not on my bucket list. I was more like St. Peter Neri, who turned down the offer of the cardinal's hat, declaring, "No, thanks. I prefer Heaven." My ambitions were humble – **to be an ordinary parish priest** in a diocese **like my great uncles**, nothing more for the moment.

Lining Up

Meanwhile, Seminary Administrators were so busy spraying the seedlings for tares and other weeds, that they failed to promote new varieties of resilient cultivars, i.e. those cool dudes, hiding in the corners of the field, who might better secure a Future for the Church in a changing world. Stymied by a narrow sectarian curriculum and with limited peer interaction, we wasted valuable time and energy pleasing the brass and avoiding expulsion, instead of meeting the world on its terms. As a matter of fact, we were **so** intimidated by our "betters," that when the aging rector at Huntington Seminary fell backward into a six-foot snow drift (after lining us up outdoors for troop inspection <u>during a blizzard</u>), none of us dared to **step out of line to** pick him up. We just left him yelling and making snow angels until a monsignor finally saved the old coot. None of us laughed. We remained as stoic as Beefeaters, lest our smiles betray a lack of respect and brand us as insubordinate. We had learned long ago to hold our tongues and curb our enthusiasm (which in my case was for philosophy) if we wanted to remain players in the game.

Waking- up

We started our priestly training as pre-teens with awe and trepidation, humbly assuming that our professors knew what they were doing and were holier and wiser than us. Yet, as I progressed, I began to wonder whether these rules and interventions were really, "All for the greater glory of God," as St. Ignatius claimed, or even out of legitimate "fatherly" concern OR, more likely, just a convenient opportunity for frustrated alpha-celibates to vent their frustrations upon lesser eunuchs (p.s. as rumor has it, some Mother Superiors were just as authoritarian).

When I entered the Major Seminary on Long Island, I started questioning the practice of the faculty searching our rooms for contraband after every home visit. Had they planted and installed undercover **customs officials** among us? Spies?

And another thing, why were we forbidden from visiting each other's rooms? (I suspect out of fear that this might foster "particular friendships," if you know what I mean.) Both practices were more than a little demeaning, making it painfully clear to us how, despite our years of showing deference and tolerating their quirks, **the faculty still didn't trust us**. As the saying goes, "Handcuffs effectively bind both slave and master, jailers and prisoners," which, I'm sure you'll agree, is a pretty sad state of affairs in an institution whose byword is love. Such practices were bound to fuel rebellion and force us to agree with **Walt Whitman** that, **"Foolish consistency is the hobgoblin of little minds." Or with Nietzche, "Disobedience – the slave's claim of nobility."**

Shush – Our Secret Weapon

Our **weapon of choice** against such institutional madness throughout my seminary career **both** in the USA and Europe was **humor** of all sorts: **Highbrow, lowbrow, and middlebrow,** whichever. For instance, **in Rome,** after we took a test on **Hans Kung's book,** "The Church," a friend of mine decided to entertain the troops with a mock lecture. He said, "Fellow scholars, after reading this exposition of the traditional teachings of the Church on Holy Orders and the papacy a la Kung, I feel that the Kung presentation was inadequate. While I concur with Professor Kung's position concerning **Apostolic Succession,** I would dare to say that **I can make a stronger case** than he does based **on strictly sociological grounds** using the tools of historical research. As you all know from historical records, whenever sacred or secular autocrats (like popes) decide to "pass on the torch," **class A** tyrants choose **class A successors** while **class B** tyrants choose a lackluster class

C syncopate as their successor. Right? Follow me now. Watch where I'm going with this! Let's just say that you begin with **the Apostles (who were not the brightest candles in the box)** and imagine this pattern of passing the torch from apostle (class B) to bishop (class C) to continue up to the present in an unbroken chain for 2000+ years. What would you expect such a practice to yield, my friends? I'll tell ya what, an inbred bunch of dog-faced, backstabbing bureaucrats, all pimped-out in Mazzetas lined with ermine and looking piously down their noses at the rest of us. You might catch them smoking "Luckies" in private, drinking shots of Villa Zarri, and renting condos along the Arno or near Naples with the money they harvested from the "All Saint's Day" collection envelopes. (Better known as **Haul Saint's Day** by those in on the take)

That said, our "lecturer" reached behind his chair for a banjo and started singing an Elvis cover rip-off by Italian pop star Bobby Solo, a tour d'force worthy of the Grand Ole Opry. We showed our appreciation with a cannonade of cat-calls, finely-crafted vulgarities, and salvos of Spumanti Corks, followed by an impromptu raid on the faculty's basement pantry via dumb waiter, (thanks to a brother with the nerve and know-how to pull that off!) It was a night to remember.

"Would you like to hear my speech in Latin?" asked the lecturer. "Heck no," we laughed and began whistling and stomping our feet in tandem. After midnight, heads dizzy from "roasting" our betters, we stumbled back to our rooms to puke and pray, hoping that the aspirin we swallowed would kick in before 5:30 a.m. morning Prayer. Ah, but it was a Grand Shindig! Still, to be honest, as Magnolia sang in "<u>Showboat</u>" **it was only "make-believe."** In the end, after the lights were dimmed and nausea subsided, we found ourselves, "alone again, naturally" as Gilbert O'Sullivan put it – satire could only sustain us so far before our alarms rang "like clockwork" to call us to chapel, morning prayer, and a day of same old, same old (or, in **our** case, 'psalm old, psalm old').

Freedom

Speaking of make-believe, I saw an iconic example of justice and vindication depicted on the screen in, 'Yankee Doodle Dandy' when James Cagney, exiled and stranded in London, pacing to and fro along a darkling pier, looked up and saw a signal rocket rise from a ship bound for New York. The flare burst in the night sky confirming that Cagney had been **cleared** of throwing the London Derby Race. In a flash, a spotlight found Cagney who laughed and shouted, "Hooray," then broke into a celebratory Jig to the tune, "Give my regards to Broadway." Later on, in the film 'The Great Escape,' I witnessed how joining with other like-minded comrades can start a movement. My cousin, Willie, used to warn me, "Don't read the comics or watch movies, you'll get **ideas**." He was right! They kept coming, and in Rome my cadre become known as 'The Dirty Dozen.'

*****

Up the road

In Italy, I would find **the venue** I needed to develop as a missionary. This didn't come in the form of an official assignment but as a willingness to go native and share the local vibes and values. Once I settled in, and I had feasted breakfast, lunch, and dinner on Italian cooking, and language, I felt ready to take chances, to do new things, and strive to become more and more awake (both politically and ecclesiastically speaking).

Breaking News: I haven't fact-checked this, but it is rumored that Pope Francis is presently considering relaxing the requirement of celibacy for some Roman Catholic priests. **If true**, I can imagine

Cardinals on dates, getting their capes dry-cleaned, trimming their whiskers, and trading in their slippers for dance shoes. Non-fraternization **had been the norm before,** the **sine qua non** in the olden days. **Now** it might be OK to invite a cute Carmelite to watch a movie **(Cine cun NUN!) and whisper,** "Keep your cowl on, sister! I'm not proposing marriage, only a private viewing of "La Notte di Cabiria" and a shot of Sambuca. SALUTE, Baby!"

"Viva el Papa e Federico Fellini!" to quote Neal Upstart, my aka.

*****

My Life as a Nerd Outside the School
Before Rome I Had Two Channels of My Enlightenment
No.1. Museum Visits in My Teens
Interpreting works of art (dialogue) (1955-1966)

Rome, my future home, was a hoarder of antiquities and an avaricious merchant eager to borrow, recycle, or outright steal the treasures, customs, and goods of conquered peoples. Most of the "Roman" statuary in the Vatican Museum are copies, offspring of Greek originals. The Christian altars in the Holy City wear the hand-me-down marble slabs that once clothed The Colosseum. The Porphyry in St. Peter's was pagan. St. Peters itself sits astride two earlier churches and its cupola is a tip of the hat to the Pantheon, which was built as a shrine to pagan gods. I, myself am not a through-bred. I'm a hand-me-down, the heir of Irish, Austrian, German, and Italian forbearers – a winning combination if I do say so myself.

A Little Overwhelmed at first

I brought to Rome cultural luggage from Brooklyn, the sainted home of the Dodgers, Aaron Copland, Barbra Streisand, and a world-famous bridge, etc. I came there as a city boy mildly conversant with the arts, that is to say, "art in fun size portions" acquired as my interest and fancy dictated. But once I set foot in ROMA, a really ancient city, I was overwhelmed as Legions of attractions assailed me from every side. I felt like an indecisive kid in a toy store trying to decide which toy to pick, crushed by choice and crying in frustration. Oh, how I missed my tranquil and leisurely walks in Prospect and Central Parks in New York which gently delivered me to my two favorite places where I could sample science and culture one gallery at a time. These were, **"The Museum of Natural History,"** which housed dinosaurs and anthropological exhibits that provoked more spiritual goosebumps and wonder in me than any church building had ever done, and the **"Brooklyn Museum of Art"** which boasted a world-class Egyptian Wing showcasing mummies in one section and the next salon, some fine examples of Babylonian statuary, both mementos of two fallen Empires, referred to as eagles in Chapter 22 of Ezekiel. The second floor housed the Americana exhibits (which I couldn't get enough of), i.e., fully restored colonial and turn-of-the-century rooms, and just down the hallway past the glassware hung the solemn 18th and 19th-century American portraits and the enormous landscape paintings of the Hudson River School. Both museums were non-threatening places to enter and visit after a stroll in the park, whereas, in Rome, the city was itself a museum whose collection ran helter-skelter through the streets, pressing me on every side and halting the excavation of subway tunnels. Very unsettling indeed! Totally other-worldly!

A self-made expert

As a teen, I had a critic's chutzpah. Despite my lack of formal training, I felt free to lecture my younger sister on what I gleaned from the paintings we visited. I remember one day in the Brooklyn Museum when we stood in front of a painting depicting a spittoon sprouting roses. I took my hint from the plaque on the frame and began, expounding, "What we have here is a metaphor - contrasting this vessel of spit and tobacco and the flowers rooted in it a pageant of color overcoming the drool and detritus of man." (I'm sure I didn't use those words. We were fifteen and fourteen, respectively).

"How do you know what the artist meant to say?" she asked. (Spoiler, this is hermeneutical question and hermeneutics is a key theme in this book.)

"Look at the title, 'Still Life'. It shows roses alive and beautiful, soaring pristinely over a pot of waste," I said.

My sister took my word as gospel until we got to the next canvas of a bowl of fruit also labeled, 'Still Life' and it dawned on both of us and we laughed. These weren't titles. They were genres.

I guess I hadn't had enough shoe leather in my diet yet, so I let myself get caught again explaining a painting by Andrew Wyeth, a yellow, brown, and white bedroom scene with an open window and diaphanous lace curtains dangling in the breeze. It was called 'The Chambered Nautilus' and I took it allegorically and said, "This little bedroom chamber open to the world, dangling its lacey filaments and feelers at the world outside its sill, etc., etc.

"What's that on the bed stand?" she asked.

"It's a shell," I snapped, "Of, yes, a **chambered nautilus.**"

I'm glad I didn't throw in a reference to Oliver Wendell Holmes's poem with the same name. Still, one grows through one's mistakes and seeks statelier mansion for one's soul, hopefully, with better appointments. After my nautilus debacle, I decided some art history was in order with courses in modern art. Thereby, building and expanding my mental gallery gradually one Braque at a time.

N.Y. Art Scene 1950s – Beyond Representational Painting

Surfing the billows of ignorance concerning Modern Art which inundated the non-Manhattan New Yorkers in the 50s, my friend Richard and I mined some laughs at the Brooklyn Museum. We came upon a small bronze statue on a pedestal with hands reaching out, turned palms up while a larger figure flowing from its heels rose behind it and arched over it. The title, no surprise, was **"Shadow."** Yep, that was a statue with a shadow alright. What else could it be unless…**unless** one placed a penny in its upturned palm? In came a man with his son, they took in the piece and the kid ran to take the penny. His father stopped him, "That's part of the statue." He read the plaque and started to lecture how money, and riches, were like a dark shadow looming over mankind. At the height of the lecture. I stepped forth, patted my shirt, said, "Oh, there you are," and pocketed the penny. The kid said to his dad, "But you said it was…." And the father scowled and pulled him away as we howled. Later the same day, we saw a space in which no painting hung but which appeared like a frame with two slim curtains forming the vertical sides and the wainscot and crown molding completing the square, creating a beautiful framed empty wall long before minimalist art was a thing. So, Richard and I started to lecture and criticize the empty space and soon a crowd joined us. As the number of onlookers grew, we slipped back behind the crowd giggling as these fools admired the latest iteration of **"The Emperor's New Clothes."** Clearly, modern art was ahead of its time for them as well as for us. Nevertheless, I eventually caught up and became a fan and true believer if not a consumer. (My mother didn't raise any fools).

****

Sylvan Guards of Honor

What do woods be speak as they silently reach year by year, ring by ring, to a vital source of energy and light? Their annual rings predate the rings of Saturn and honor living God of living things.

"Split a piece of wood and I am there," says Christian in a gnostic gospel and so say Druids, mystics, converts, and process theologians. The height and depth of creation and prologue of St. John with a full-throated, "Amen."

What say ye? Knock on wood (moan).

The Forrest Spoke

Art Scandal in Venice (1968)
A Horse and Rider Statue

At the entrance of the Guggenheim Art Museum in Venice stands a controversial statue just begging for a creative interpreter like me. To come along in front of this affrontery stood a stodgy British matron who after reading the inscription "Angel o the city" by Marino Martini, exclaimed, "What was Peggy Guggenheim thinking placing this nasty thing on display? What's wrong with these Americans anyway."

"Excuse me, madam," I interjected. "But the British share some responsibility with that nursery rhyme."

"Which one?" she asked.

"You know, ride a cock horse to Bombay Cross."

"Good Lord," she exclaimed and departed, leaving me curious to see what else was inside. Google the statue if you must.

******

Channel No.2
The Botanical Garden-my left Brain
Intercranial Civil War
Science vs Asthetics

Nature is a haunted house but Art is a house that tries to be haunted (E. Dickinson)

Which to favor-Science or Aesthetics?

How many flowers

Or Perish on the Hill

Without the privilege to know

That they are Beautiful

(E. Dickinson)

Beauty is not caused-it is

Chase it and it ceases -

chase it not-and it abides-

(nesting in the creases)

A sacred moment

"One fine day the trees whispered the word 'Being' to me (a metaphysical epiphany granted to an agnostic philosopher **Jacques Maritan** upon his conversion). In my humble opinion, what he heard that day was the voice of "the **forest primeval**, the murmuring pines and the hemlocks" gently attempting to **Evangelize him**.

I philosophize

*Plato warns not to philosophize before age 50. But he's dead.

I was 15, a high school sophomore at the time (sophomore, as you know, means lover of wisdom) and I sat translating my Latin copy of <u>Ovid</u>, with my back propped against a tree and the book in my lap. This spot was my Walden Pond, my Fresh Air Retreat Center.

After a while, I decided to take a break. As I looked around, a thought occurred to me, "**Colors, why are there so many**?" Some of which are even invisible to the naked eye. How did God, a spirit with no eyes, come up with inventing color and creating a stained-glass world like ours? He must be even more anthropocentric than Prometheus or perhaps He planned on visiting us someday and would enjoy witnessing "in living color" the blush of surprise on our faces. I imagine that St. Peter was also blushing when he said to Our Lord, "Depart from me, for I am a sinful man." Or when Christ asked, "Do you love me?"

Even the co-discoverer of evolution by natural selection was awed by color. He wrote, "The beauty of butterfly wings and bird plumage so exceeds the demands of 'utility' in biological nature that one is moved to consider a theological rationale, namely that they are there for human enjoyment of the 'Greatest show on earth.'"(Alfred Russel Wallace p.94 from "Keys to Balthasar")

For the moment, this was just a mind game on my part, a mental query like the musical one raised by a trumpet in Charles Ives, "Unanswered Question" which causes the other horns to debate, builds to a cacophony and ends with a Joycian-like shrug by the coronet, 'Wha, wha, wha, wha,' and finally concludes in silence (Am I being too pretentious? Of course, I am! But not off the mark).

Back then, I knew nothing of Meister Echhart's quote linking God and color i.e. that "**God is green** and flowering **in his spiritual power**" nor the meaning of his mysterious claim, "The eye with which I see God is the same eye with which He sees me." Ah, those mystics. Their words slake our deepest thirst for God with tankards scooped in pearl, "full of a brew that is true" (Princess Bride).

And so, **moving on,** I refocused my attention on a mundane little footbridge in the garden that stretched across this noisy brook full of bubbles, moss-bearded stones, tadpoles, and some fish. **This 'bridge over bubbling waters' raised the question**: where did the stream come from? Was this stream fed by an aquifer like the stream between the subway tracks i.e. dredged to accommodate groundwater? No! Subway waters are dark and lifeless! This stream was crystalline and life-supporting, maybe flowing from an audacious artesian well that defied the impasse of pavement and apartments to bubble up and sustain this demi-paradise. I jumped to my feet to find out if the miracle was caused by nature or human design and followed the brook to the point where the garden met the pavement. **What did I find?** A pair of fire hydrants gushing water full blast. Was this the source of all this inner-city wonder? My God, the wizard behind all these **natural** wonders turned out to be a lowly city planner from the Parks Department. I shouldn't have been crestfallen but I was! After all, isn't it the nature of gardens to be both created and maintained by human beings, a Nexus of beauty and technology, the collaboration of cultivators and aqueducts, trellises and pruners, a left and right brain victory? Randomly pitting one against the other inevitably produces in one some cognitive dissonance, a case of the 'willies.' A needless war of the worlds.

Still, as a New Yorker and a bit of a romantic, there is nothing like a hydrant to flush away the joy and faux spontaneity of finding a rose garden watered by fire plugs in a concrete jungle. Years later in Czechoslovakia, I witnessed this very anomaly again – a delicious surprise at the end of a drab urban street in Prague that opened to reveal the **VRTBA, a terraced** Italian Garden which it had deliciously concealed.

But, back then, as a teenager in Brooklyn, as I said, I was incapable of sustaining unqualified Wonder, without cynicism intruding and spoiling the fun. Sadly, I just let my Brooklyn ambivalence get the best of me as I exited the Botanical Gardens crestfallen and reverted to seeing the world through **amber-colored glasses** instead of those rose-colored ones designed for viewing Wonderlands unambiguously. One might say, I was caught with my Pan pipes down.

Looking back sixty years later, after reading the late philosophical writings of Martin Heidegger concerning **the Greek concept of "Physics"** or "nature," I wouldn't have bothered to investigate the humble origin of the stream. I'd simply, imbibed the beauty-at-hand and followed the ecstasies back to 'Being Itself' whose givenness and giving-ness captivates artists and thinkers willing to disappear into the actuality of the moment and concede with Karl Jaspers, "A rose is not a thing; it is a performance to be enjoyed." (Too flowery?)

*****

Challenge of Faith
Three Steps Forward
"God is within us like the sun is in the color and the fragrance of a flower." These are the words of blind Helen Keller, blessed are those who have not seen and yet believe.

I critique

Institutional blindness 101

While the garden's engineers were ingenious enough to solve the irrigation problem by piping in water from the Catskill Mountains to Johnny Pump, its plan designer lacked both creativity and sensitivity. The first thing one sees when entering the Botanical Gardens is, in no way, one of the "seven wonders of the world." It is **a prosaic herb and spice collection.** Not very inspiring. I have grown several of these plants in my kitchen window box. So, I shrugged, plucked a peppermint leaf to chew on, and moved on to the first main attraction, i.e. the model "Japanese Garden" replete with stone carved lanterns with pagoda hats, a covered boat landing where one could step out and observe koi mindfully swimming, and of course, the tranquil lake itself that bordered the narrow pathway through the garden proper. All this was located on the right side of the path. But up the road, to the left, and behind some bushes, was the entrance to a subdivision housing a special circle of waist-high planters brimming with touchable and sweetly scented plants selected to delight the blind visitor who could read the braille labels and smell and feel the greenery. The visually challenged then could make the rounds and exit on the path a few meters across from the lake, whereupon the blind spots of the planner's design became apparent and perilous. These craftsmen had created a garden that was definitely 'of the sighted, by the sighted and only for the sighted.' One could only hope that the last braille entry was written **in Big Bold Dots** recommending a sharp left turn back to the path or else the next plant the blind would feel would be duckweed and the next flower they huffed might be a koi, thereby, leaving the groundskeeper **no choice** but to gather up their white canes off the surface of the pond and shake his head. "Poor victims. You should have visited the zoo." A better choice indeed! Simon and Garfunkel claim, "Everything (you need) is happening at the zoo." (Provided that you don't poke the gorilla with your white cane or pet a yawning hippo). So, for the visually impaired, I would say:

If you haven't got a snorkel and some flippers,

You should check out all the offerings at the zoo.

They have sounds and odors there to please the senses that remain,

And no deathtrap made of duckweed to wade through.

I Theologize

Nuns in the USA as Mentors - Part 1

In the States, and throughout my life (an occupational hazard) **nuns played a major role** in my primary education and the discernment of my religious vocation. When I was only three years old, a clingy, timid, and obedient child with attachment issues, the only women I had ever kissed were my mom and a statue of the Madonna filled with rosary beads. One afternoon while my mother and I were going to church, I released her hand and ran to a nun wearing rosary beads and a large cross on her hip (talk about the best of two worlds!) I grabbed her by the **crucifix**, kissed it, and looking up **I smiled and crowed, "God."** Whether I meant by that Jesus or Father God or Cupid, only Freud can say. All I know is that it was a case of "adoration" at first sight. I learned that nuns were approachable, safe, and nice. I revised that opinion later during the reign of terror conducted by the Sisters of Mercy (don't let the title fool you) who taught me in St. Jerome's Parochial School, Flatbush, Brooklyn N.Y.

My next encounter with nuns was when I and two of my siblings worked with the **Nursing Sisters of the Sick Poor** (actual title) as teenagers. It was my first missionary experience and it coincided with a crisis of faith. The nuns ran a camp for the mentally handicapped during the summer and I was a counselor several summers in a row. But while doing good work, I was wrestling with a question raised by a seminary professor. "How do you know you are praying to the true God or not just one of your fantasies like Santa or the Easter Bunny?" I took it to heart!

I had no idea that our spiritual director was merely serving up a philosophical chestnut left over from his reading of Hume and Feuerbach (we hadn't studied philosophy yet). But how could **I** answer the question? Well, I thought, how do we virtually encounter others from afar? I knew, for instance, that you'd only have to play me three measures of Aaron Copeland, for him to become as present to me as when he signed me a copy of his opera, "Second Hurricane" at the Record Hunter, Fifth Avenue N.Y. Or just recite two lines from a poem by Dickinson and I'd be immediately transported to the windowsill of her parlor and share vistas through her sharper eyes. But of course, we're talking about **artists**. Unlike us commoners who often muddy the waters to appear profound, artists prop their inimitable souls on the petard of a pen through which they facilitate a spirit-to-spirit connection with the uninspired reader. So, why not submit what the Evangelist words to the same "spiritual" litmus test? That's exactly what I did.

I read St. John and St. Paul every evening and strained to hear the thunderous gravitas of **their Master's voice** coaching, guiding, and infusing their writings with extraordinary life and singularity. I hoped that the same dynamism that inspired them to write would empower my work in summer camp with a zeal beyond my resources. Finally, **I felt God in word and deed and I believed**! He called me in the shallows and met me in the depths (Jonn, 21). It wasn't through rigorous Cartesian doubt but by the logic of the heart. I followed the dots and they led to the nib of a divine stylus and a message addressed to me personally. **G.K.**

Chesterton wrote, "There is a road from the eye to the heart that does not go through the intellect. **Let your religion be less theory** and **more a love affair**." Good enough for the moment, although, later on, when I did get to study philosophy and apologetics, I enjoyed adding understanding to conviction.

And murmured to myself, "Up your ante son of sem!"

*****

A laborer in the vineyard

No Coward Soul Is Mine

No Trembler in the world's storm-troubled sphere

I see Heaven's glories shine (and sense)

God within my breast…

With wide-embracing love

(C. Bronte)

<u>I serve</u>

Though **all the baptized** are called to mission, not all are called to be **field hands.** Our response and readiness may vary. Some sign the covenant tentatively i.e., "Yours to a certain degree!" Others "go the whole hog," "tail to snout," "Forever Yours, Lord."

While I was working with the nursing sisters (cir.1960), during one of the happiest and most blessed summers to date, something strange occurred. The director, Fr. Cribbin, sent a priest to say Mass for the campers. Everyone was pumped up including a Goliath of a man with

Down syndrome who was anxious to show the "father" his helmet, a gift from a local firehouse. The priest appeared on the ground and **Goliath lumbered toward him**, groaning "Father, Father." **The priest backed away** until he was pressed against the hurricane fence shouting, "Help!" In an instant, a waif of a counselor raced to the rescue, grabbed Goliath by the hand, and led him away from the priest screaming, "Get over here, you're scaring the Father." The priest bolted, leaving his stole on the ground like the sheet left by the naked man fleeing the Garden of Olives and I watched **innocence in a helmet** meander away crying, led by the firm and familiar hand of a loving volunteer. He was a Christ figure if ever I saw one (with downcast eyes as soulful as those of the beaten mare in <u>Crime and Punishment</u>).

Part II

Bon Voyage!

1967

On the day of my departure to Italy, my family gathered at the dock where the Michelangelo, flagship of the Italian line, was anchored. We exchanged goodbyes and I promised my mom that I'd tell her how the food on board was compared to grandma's cooking. **The Michelangelo was huge**. It looked like the Chrysler Building lying on its side with the forearm of a gangplank resting on the quay palm side up. Even sideways, the ship towered over us, aloof and offsetting, having none of the charm of our beloved Staten Island Ferry with its corona of salt sea spray, gulls circling, and those special treats like big soft pretzels, dirty water franks and cheers of the passengers when the captain threw the engines in reverse causing pylons to creak and complain as the ferry kissed the shore. Reluctantly, I picked up my suitcase and boarded the monster already missing my people. Having never left home before, it broke my heart to see them (my former life) appear so small and insignificant when viewed from the upper deck of this ocean liner. The last time I was aboard a boat it was with them on our **Circle Line touring around Manhattan Island**. The boat crashed midway and mid-channel, its canopy decapitated by the bridge raining shards of steel and plastic down upon us. We struggled to extricate my grandma, Uncle Al, and Aunt Hilda out from under the folding chairs while the boat floated backward towards the embankment, mounted it stern first, and then slid back into the river with ominous rasping noises. Luckily, some boys on the shore saw us, dove in, grabbed the ropes, and secured us. The company gave us coupons for another ride! Fat chance! I'd as soon book a canoe ride over Niagara Falls. They say if you deploy your paddles as wings for the last 500 ft, you'll land like a swan. No, thanks. My mother didn't raise any fools!

Standing now on another deck, my brain was blank, barely taking in the sights and sounds around me, all at once, the hammer fell – it was **trauma time again**! The deck shook, the seal holding us close to the pier gave way, blackwater opened between boat and shore, whistles wailed, tug horns belched, children were startled and clung to their parents and I thought, "Sorry kids, they can't help you now." **Then my mind started playing clips from old newsreel footage** about disasters at sea, narrated by sepia tone announcers in hysteric detail. (Have I told you how old things frightened me back then: the smell of old wood, rubber, cloth, and cartons, dust-covered phonograph records, ancient magazines, in short, those denizens of attics bequeathed to us from people who knew them as new but now, in an altered state, these same objects represented mortality and death itself to their heirs). They were my childhood terrors. Nowadays, I collect antiques as a hobby. Go figure! Call it resignation or letting God be God.

Recovering my wits, I tried to take solace in the fact that there were no bridges to crash into between America and Europe, only open sea. Open sea? Enough! I let go of the rail and staggered to my cabin and let the waves rock me to sleep.

The following morning arrived with hope and curiosity. Hope for Italian food like mia nonna's and I was curious to see my shipmates, the scholarship winners from other states. Unfortunately, it was a double disappointment. The waiters served an American-style breakfast and I found myself seated across from two guys from Indiana with broad smiles and horse teeth. It felt as if I had mistakenly wandered into a set of Twilight Zone and was sitting down to a meal with Edgar Bergan's famous lap-pal dummies asking them, "Could you pass the sawdust, please?" Yet, "mirabile dictu" we gradually hit it off. Friends for life. Thank God! "Menos mal." If I couldn't bond with guys from other states, what chance would it take to break "pane" with "gli Romani?" The Romans.

Throughout the voyage, I was amazed to see how our backgrounds dictated our activities aboard the ship. The eastern seminarians played shuffleboard and remained in clusters. The mid-westerners won dance contests and were deadly shots at skeet. I thought to myself, **which group was better suited for ministry, the cloistered** or **the cool? I made my** choice – **Rumspringa** all the way. Game on!

*****

My European Home
My Impressions of the Pontifical Gregorian University

I don't remember what happened when we landed. I did notice that compared to the White House, St. Peter's exterior looked dirty. The Gregorian University was just as disappointing – somber, packed with soiled cassocks and unkempt students, and sounding like a Turkish Bizarre when 35 mother tongues exploded all at once between classes. I used to get terribly bus-sick riding there in the morning and even sicker drinking espresso on an empty stomach. So, I switched to a banana and a cappuccino then popped an occasional Dramamine and I was good to go.

How was this student body vetted? Well, America sent her best there to study but, pardon my jingoism, other countries were more democratic. The Italians had the edge over us in the beginning since we couldn't read the crib notes they passed around during exams but we gained traction after a year to meet and bet the best of them. Looking left to right it was hard to believe that Greg was the alma mater of saints and popes.

In my **third year**, I heard rumors of a **scandal** involving some Greg students. Maybe some of the notes they were passing during testing included the addresses and phone numbers of some women. In any case, I learned that an entire class from the Mexican College and their teacher had been arrested and sent back to Mexico after cavorting with ladies at the baths of Caracalla. Wow! My friends and I had just been there to see a production of "Aida" (which included real live horses. Yeah) and we considered that a wild **night on the town.** I still can't believe that our Latino brethren actually decided to go there as a class to horse around. Talk about school spirit! Anyhow, as the saying goes, "Different strokes for different folks." and, I imagine their rejoinder to be "When in Rome do like the Romans do." Case closed! I can hear them mumbling under their breath "Thank you, Emperor Caracalla (A.D.206.) for baths with benefits. Andale, Andale! Vamos!"

North American College (NAC) Our Residence

Our residence, North American College which was known as the **"boot camp for American Bishops,"** was situated on Gianicolo Hill overlooking the Eternal City. It was a gated community sitting on a choice piece of property with a concierge, a staff of waiters and groundskeepers, many of who lived with their families on the property, and a convent of nuns who lived within the compound and did the cooking and laundry. The Rector was a tall ruddy angular-faced bishop who I'll nickname Big Red. He was in charge of operations, ineptly assisted by a Vice-Rector, two spiritual directors, and several postgraduate priests who acted as handlers for hundreds of student seminarians in their chronological twenties.

Rules

The rules were few: attend the university, **earn your degree**, worship, give your superiors respect and obedience, and **don't bother the nuns**. We were afforded greater freedom here than we had in the States. Here you could visit rooms, congregate, have visitors, and act as tour guides for people coming from your state, etc. Still, the mentality of **the faculty** had not hit a refresh button in years, not because the world hadn't changed but because they were intimidated by the legend of Pandora and the fragility of their positions. **Their cardinal rules** were twofold, **"keep the lid on the box"** and **"steady the boat."** Despite their vigilance, things were unraveling at North American College in 1966. The two spiritual directors, (in charge of 280 students) Monsignors Galles and Holleran, reported that many students blamed the seminary for difficulties in their spiritual and personal lives and both directors fired back that the fault rested squarely on the students for their lack of dedication to and fulfillment in the "system." (Aggiornamento p.260). So, much for positive thinking, guys! Still, I'll grant them this – they were sharp enough to notice that many of us did not embrace the church as an institution. Rather, we saw ourselves as burgeoning professionals in training. My class arrived in 1967, the same year that **Aretha Franklin** recorded the song, 'Respect.' Just a little bit of respect was all we were asking for and Aretha **was our spokesperson**.

****

Behold, The Summer of Our Discontent

That year storm clouds gathered at the gates of North American College with a visit of a "radical" priest, **Fr. Daniel Berragan**, a protestor of the Vietnam War. He met with some North American students who reported afterward, "His concrete witness gave us pause to reflect." And reflect they did, as to what style of priesthood could best manage the challenges of the times. The words of Bob Dylan's "Ballad of a Thin Man" rang painfully true in the circumstances, **"Something is happening here and you don't know what it is. Do you, Mr. Jones**?" Log by log the stockades protecting the faculty from the changing world outside were being dismantled. Our faculty never imagined that a concept like "built-in obsolescence," which applied to things like cars and clothes in the secular world might also apply to the church structures as creatures of time. In the face of change, history records how the ancient Venetians threw up their hands and wailed, **"You can't teach an old Doge new tricks,"** a belief they maintained throughout the tenure of **120 doges (rulers)** spanning 1100 years. It took a coup by an outsider, Napoleon, to cut the silk cords and send their Morano chandeliers crashing to the palace floor. (Too poetic?) Well, the faculty of NAC had their **brand of Venetian blindness** as regards their outmoded traditions, pyrite pretensions, and fashions that became fixtures, for example, vintage clothing (albs and cassocks), Latin liturgies and a college of red-caped cardinals who once were ambassador-princes. But nowadays, there are no 'Kings' left to visit, 'Your Lordships.' And so, as tide and time hum, "Que sera, sera."

As the leaf subsides into a leaf

As Eden sank into grief

And the day goes down to a day, face it, friends

Nothing 'gold' can stay. (R. Frost)

Our faculty continued to employ practices in vogue in **their** seminary days, while we students found **our** inspiration and values in mainstream culture which celebrated youth, freedom, and liberal causes in songs such as Bob Dylan's iconic, "The Times They Are A Changing" and the Seekers' announcement: "There's a new world somewhere, they call the Promised Land," and of course, Phil Oaks's "Canons of Christianity." To be honest, **all of us** seminarians (every last one of us) **were raised as religious conservatives**, cut from the same traditional cloth **as our parents**. We came to Rome to study and become traditional priests, while being men of the '60s, more likely to be fans of Woodstock than Bayreuth, more likely to think of ourselves as owls perched **temporarily** on the rafters of the "Pontifical Gregorian University" and **eyeing** a **religious** not a **teaching career**. In short, my class leaned more towards town and pulpit than to cap and gown. Smart cookies, though, these schoolmates of mine. As for myself, I was the crossover nerd baptized, reconfigured, a new-age Christian on the Michelangelo Ocean Liner.

Why the priesthood?

I vaguely remember **one early challenge** to my vocational choice years before arriving in Italy. It came from my grandmother's adopted son, a Jewish dry goods merchant who, when he heard that I might go to Rome, asked me why I would even consider joining such a conservative

63

organization like the Catholic Church. He didn't get it. For me the answer was obvious! I was signing up with the **only authentic Church in Christendom** for which I was prepared to give up family, private bank accounts, and freedom in exchange for serving God. All of my classmates believed this. We didn't come to Rome to "take the doors off the jams and the jams off the wall," (Alan Ginsburg) but to be priests. We were good guys, honor students, eager to learn and hoping to study under great professors who could enrich our understanding of faith and raise it to the next level. **We had been told since high school seminary that one learned math to prepare for philosophy and philosophy to prepare for theology and theology for the priesthood.** Rome was the last link in the chain. Rome, the Eternal City, the dead center of the Catholic world, was our spiritual and educational destination until given our first parish assignments. Yes, my classmates and I held all this in common. However, as to lifestyles and tastes, we were a motley crew.

Who were we?

In broad strokes, the class of 1967 was divided into **two camps**: the liberals numbered 30% led by the infamous 'dirty dozen.' The other 70% were the company men who whined a lot about rules and restrictions but who weren't ready to burn the building down. They just towed the line, and bided their time, hoping to warm their hands with chestnuts plucked from the liberals' auto-da-fe! (a safe bet)

Did prayer and liturgy bring this diverse but pious community together, you may ask? Unfortunately, not! Almost all of us missed the contemporary liturgies **(folk masses)** we enjoyed **in the US** but, truth be told, our liturgy in Rome began as an embarrassment. Take, for example, the sheer sentimentalism of this Marian oldie:

"Bring flowers of the fairest

Bring flowers of the rarest,

from garden and woodland and hillside and dale.

Our full hearts are swelling,

Our glad voices telling,

the praise of the loveliest rose of the vale.

O Mary, we crown thee with blossoms today,

Queen of the angels, Queen of the May, etc."

Shrugs of the shoulders

What in the world? **There's enough syrup here** to turn a haystack into a sticky bun! Oh, how we longed for the toe-tapping, hand-clapping folk masses we enjoyed in the States, and the privileges and the recognition we enjoyed there as honor students. Respect! R.E.S.P.E.C.T. We weren't Adlerians. Respect meant a lot to us.

So, when my class arrived in 1967, the agents-of-change among us focused on being granted two concessions as a welcoming gesture from the institution to her grade-A candidates: **1st, eliminating the dress code, and 2nd, eliminating the curfew**. This was bad news for the faculty with divided loyalties who had both to serve us and to give account for policy changes to old-guard bishops and cardinals. Like it or not, NAC's Pax Romana had finally come to an end for our handlers.

Why? "For the times, they are a'changing."

****

Target 1: The Cassock

Like all the other national colleges, e.g. the Irish College, the African College, the Mexican, etc., all seminarians in the city were required to wear the cassock inside and outside the college walls - the various styles and colors (school colors) proclaimed the wearer's nationality. The conservatives among us liked wearing them in public. They liked to dress up and march around town like junior bishops. The rest of us were men of the '60s and questioned the purpose and advisability of cassocks. They didn't serve a liturgical function outside the wall. They weren't a sign of ecclesiastical status – we weren't ordained yet. No, they were merely schoolboy uniforms or summer camp T-shirts, nothing more. Furthermore, couldn't **cassocks** possibly have a **negative political and sociological impact on the people of the city**, inciting anticlerical and xenophobic resentment upon seeing us parading, privileged, and brazen around the town? Lo and behold, we discovered that our fears were grounded in reality. Rome was the hub of religious orders, diplomats, visiting clergy, etc., in numbers exceeding the ranks of local parish priests and this imbalance did indeed foster anticlericalism. Hell's bells! As a result, the Romans called anyone wearing a cassock a "bacarozzo," which is a cockroach. And so, it certainly behooved my class to drop the offending garment and go for plain clothes. Which we did. As a result, the populace saw us as young men far from home and taking pity, adopted some of us as quasi-long-lost relatives. **Tom Kirshberg and I were taken in by the Pignatelli family** and spent many an evening at their house talking, eating pasta asciutta a la Mima, Nando's wife, and drinking wine. That made Mima happy because our drinking put the brakes on Nando's tendency to overindulge. A good time could be had by all in moderation. We were as welcome as Jesus at the marriage of Cana and Nando could tell his tales without slurring his speech.

"Thank you, Jesus."

Target 2: The Timeclock

Next on the chopping block was the curfew imposed partly for our protection but mostly to avoid institutional liability. By 10:00 pm, all good seminarians were expected to be in the compound ready for night prayers. Unfortunately, this was not always possible or desirable and **it forced us to scale the college walls.** That was a workable solution for the more athletic and adventurous brethren but after **one of us fell in front of the Main Gate** with wine bottles tucked under his jacket, our college made the Headlines, the Rector was dismissed and our soccer game attendance kept pace with our notoriety. Our **next step** was **to steal and distribute the gate keys** of the college to all the other students. The faculty countered by posting an all-night concierge and **a sign-in ledger.** We countered by entering pseudo names "to protect the insolent." This practice came to a sorry end when the rector proclaimed to the entire student body these fatal words, **"Gentlemen, I am convinced** that Mickey Mouse and Albert Einstein are one and the same." He couldn't stop the laughter. Evidently, I wasn't the only Mickey Mouse in the building and the "signing in" rule was considered a joke to all but the Rector.

Also, The Curriculum

One valuable takeaway that I garnered on the Michelangelo trip was observing how easily the guys from the Midwest blended with the other passengers on the ship. They had a folksy charisma for sure but would it filter through the brand of theological training we were about to receive at the University and enhance or cramp their style and mine? Unfortunately, my fears were realized in spades. **The courses at the Greg were dry and traditional,** a mix of Church History and Denzinger entries, as unappetizing as the Q&A of the Baltimore Catechism which we memorized in grammar school. Granted these studies were weightier, more complicated, and broken into tracts e.g. Revelation, Grace, Moral Theology, etc. but the expectation was the same - to memorize and defend them. I mused that were I ever to become a successful preacher and evangelist, I needed more marketable material than this **bloodless dance of scholastic syllogisms** offered at the Greg.

No wonder this sent seminarians like me running desperately to the works of the New theologians both for a breath of fresh air and relief from the smell of formaldehyde on Jesuit robes, the clicking of their dentures, and those old coffee stains on their lecture notes. (Ok, we did have some good ones like Fuchs and Stanley). When we discovered that we **were,** in fact, slated to be trained to become <u>caretakers of a museum</u> of musty thoughts, with no new exhibits and no fertile vineyard to tend on the weekends, we protested

"Where's our GARDENS Teacher?" we shouted.

"Quiet in the library!" they answered.

Frustrated, some of the more radical among us started looking around for outlets. Guess what we saw? Gardens needing cultivation just OUTSIDE the college gates, **mission fields ripe for harvest** in plain view nesting quietly among the pines of Rome! So, we picked up rakes and shovels and got to work.

Settling in

During the first couple of months, I got the skinny from upperclassmen, learned the routine, got measured for my casket, sorry, for my cassock, and made friends with the men in my hall. We were eyeballed by the brass, issued books and IDs, politely ate what was put before us, drank the wine (rated common) that they served daily and we learned who to go to if we got diarrhea or the flu. Many a night I thought, "Oh God, what have I gotten myself into?" Our classes were in **Latin** and even though I had 8 years of it under my belt, I was only used to reading it to myself or from a textbook in class **so switching to Latin lectures was a challenge**, to say the least. I didn't understand a thing for six months, not even chapter and verse when the professor cited passages in the Bible. And **talk about those accents**: French Latin, Spanish Latin, German Latin, American Latin, etc, spoken like an Italian Cicero, a Gallic

Julius Caesar, a Brooklyn Pliny. Oy vey! While outside the classroom, ah, the music of Italy filled the streets, beautiful Italian, the language my grandmother cursed in and which I longed to master rather than fritter away all my downtime indoors talking to other Americans at NAC. Luckily, I found an answer to my imprisonment in the person of an upperclassman named **Patrick**, the only seminarian who did ministry among the Romans before we arrived. Through him, I met an order of socially liberal but otherwise traditional nuns, **the Order of Magdalena Aulina**, who wore regular street clothing, instead of the habit and passed inoffensively among the poor. This discovery would fill my days and soul with joy and energy in the years that followed. I will refer to them as the **Spanish Nuns from Barcelona**.

Lectures vs Action

To my horror, I also discovered an enormous black hole in our priestly preparations in Rome, i.e., **no pastoral training** appeared **in our syllabus**, **not even basic courses in social work practice** which admittedly might be difficult to craft for a multinational institution like the Greg. On the other hand, who in their right mind would ask student surgeons to proceed seamlessly from lecture hall to actual practice without some mandatory cadaver carving? I'd sooner check into a city hospital with the unsavory name of Hack-n-Sack Hospital (New Jersey) than go under the scalpel of a virgin surgeon with a Harvard sheepskin. I wondered, "Did our theological professors actually expect future pastors to sit comfortably in lecture halls and libraries for four years while callously ignoring the needs of people outside the buildings?" Even **Carrivaggio**, a murderer, must have drawn from **some ponds of empathy** within him in order to execute a work like the **"Seven Acts of Mercy"** with **credibility**! Pay a visit to Naples and judge for yourself if there aren't authentic Christian sensitivities at work in those brushstrokes. Similarly, besides gaining academic diplomas, I believe that future pastors need to accrue some moral capital by serving the poor while still in training. To tell the truth, I would have liked to have our Rector and Vice Rector, who were not murderers as far as we know, go on a pilgrimage to Naples and learn from Caravaggio about mercy. I'd pay for the ticket and gladly send them off with a fond and hardy **"Va fa Napoli."**

Update: Surprise! In Bishop Barron's publication Evangelizing Culture Issue 16 page 127, I read that our pioneering outreach which was summarily condemned in the 60s has since been adopted and legitimized. NAC now assigns mandatory pastoral work to first-year students!

Acid test

My missionary metal was put to the test the very first year in Rome, after I heard that, because of famine and lack of jobs in the south of the country, (Have you seen the movie Bread and Chocolate?) Hoards of hungry families were arriving en masse in boxcars to Rome to protest that the supplies weren't being distributed. So, I joined the volunteers who manned a **soup kitchen** operating out of St. Paul's Episcopal Church within The Wall. There was also a St. Paul's Basilica outside the Wall, a Catholic Basilica that opted to do nothing for these starving families! Ironically, this would be the very church where Pope John XXIII first announced his plans for Vatican II. My charitable work was construed as **"Political Involvement"** by the faculty, so they pulled my first vacation as punishment. (spoiler alert - I took it anyway). But really, what could they do to me? Throw me out? My bishop back home wouldn't allow it. He was a big fan of kitchens and soups judging from his girth. Our rector had previously told me that I was gifted and coming from a big diocese, I was destined to "go places."

"Yeah," I said, "Back to Brooklyn."

In the end, I was allowed to stay in Rome where I met many kindred spirits in town involved in works of charity in the city and I decided to join them once I learned Italian.

****

Visiting Our Neighbors
The Challenge of the Poor
(Pope Francis urges that outreach start at the peripheries)(Open p.25)

In a shanty settlement of corrugated tin hovels clustered in the Prenestino-Labicano quarter of Rome, the **Order of Mother Teresa of Calcutta** was hard at work. Most of the nuns hailed from balmy climes like Malta where their thin habits (which resembled blue and white kitchen towels) might have afforded sufficient protection against the elements but not here in Rome in wintertime. Adjacent to these "villas miserias" stood a Vatican-sponsored housing project. Since jobs were hard to come by, those who owned apartments there, chose to rent them out for income. Even today, there are people in the outskirts of Venice who do the same but for monetary gains, i.e., they gladly choose to live modestly outside the city and sublet their ancestral holdings of canals, facades, bricoles, in a word "ambiance," to the rich and famous. However, unlike the poor in Prenestino, they earn a pretty penny (or Lira or euro) in the bargain.

Mother Teresa's nuns lived and toiled shoulder to shoulder with the poor. Their sisterly poverty served as an indictment against many religious orders who ignored marginalized people as well as against clergy who felt comfortable leaving the poor to fend for themselves. To me, that sounds more like Stoicism than Christianity. The future **Pope**

Francis agrees! He publicly **condemned** such **clerical exceptionalism** when he witnessed it firsthand in Argentina in the 60s.

Ask the Missionaries of Charity or the Spanish nuns why they **gave up their lives in Malta and Barcelona** respectively to work with the poor in Italy. I'm sure they would respond as the disciples did when questioned about stealing a donkey for Jesus to march into Jerusalem. Why? **"Because the Master needs it."** Or as **Meister Eckhart** put it, "Don't you know that **Love has no why."** I am equally impressed by Pope Francis' affirmation that "**Jesus i**s not just partying in heaven." In the Epistle to the Hebrews, he is said to be interceding, showing the Father his wounds, and **his wounds are the faces of the suffering in which he sees himself**. "It is not a pious little tale," says Pope Francis, "It is the pure and real and up-to-date truth" (Open p.31). That's a proclamation sermon right there! I don't believe Christ's wounds will heal until all have entered heaven.

My one regret of that first year was that I didn't know about the life and works of **Philip Neri,** the Apostle of Rome who worked with the poor. Granted, he was **a Theological Conservative,** (I'm not) but his earthy sense of humor and love for the poor could have made him our patron saint. He lovingly set the saintly bar low for his listeners by saying, **"Try to be good if you can."** That's **not a very Jesuit-like proverb** for sure! Be that as it may, if we had known about him while in Rome his winsome example might even have inspired us to create an Oratory of our own and buttress our activism with a proportional prayer life. I realize now that "He who does not know the face of God in contemplation, will not know it in action." I should have learned that from my summer camp experience as a teenager helping the mentally challenged **and supporting** my works **with prayer** and scripture readings.

****

72

Rome
Absorbing the City and Vice Versa (1967)

Six months after I arrived in Rome, I experienced an awakening. I was on my way to the Greg, hanging on the strap on the # 64 bus between two women who were staunch non-believers in the benefits of deodorant or mouthwash when suddenly a shiver and chill came over me. I read the room for clues and reasons for this reaction but found none. Through the bus window, **Victor Emmanuel Monument** looked back at me with indifference, and then I suddenly realized what had happened; **I had let my guard down**! I was no longer an observer. I was part of the scene, surrounded and outnumbered by real things and people, a world I would inhabit for the next four years. It was time to shed the armor, declare a truce, and read the terms of peace. No more privileges of infancy - a free and daily diet of worms minced and served me by the beak of Mother Church. I was a young eagle in training to become a Church leader. But, once the shock had passed, I was filled with a joy that the seminary days in the U.S. had never given. Yes, **I started to enjoy this Italian carnival and began to live the lifestyle of the rich and famous –** wine and waiters at the college, sightseeing every day, the freedom to relieve myself in public urinals affixed to the side of buildings Gene Kelly style. Just singing and peeing in the lane. Here I was able to access the trinity of delights of pasta, wine, and female attention (nuns) which Mother Church graciously swapped in exchange for celibacy. Senta, senta, Senore Johann Strauss Jr. Pen me a waltz per favore! Adesso, a waltz and make it presto. **I'm in love with La Bella Citta** (the beautiful city).

The very next day, I saw an apparition, reminiscent of a hummingbird. It was a lasting impression that took but a second. A lightning "touche" then a quick getaway. That's how I'd describe this nun on a scooter racing past me, traveling full throttle, leaning into her ride as she pressed forward, her habit blowing in the wind. She was a young girl, probably my age, wearing green-tinted mirror glasses. So, I said to myself in the words of Cicero, "O tempora, O mores (Oh what time and lifestyles we live in). Oh well! This is too good to let pass. This deserves a poem. So, I consulted my Horace scope, summoned my muse, and wrote this in a scrapbook:

Blow a ciao to the sands of the Hamptons

And farewell to the gulls in her bay

Since the curves of the nun on a Vespa in Rome

Sure, did nudge other pleasures away

When her mirrored sunglasses pitched my way

How I prayed they were hiding a wink

that suggested I travel to an alternate highway

And flush priestly plans down the sink. (Me)

I'm just playing! At this stage of my life, I had never been on a date, never guided a shapely waist around a dance floor. The nun was real. The rest was a dream. There was no scrapbook, no notebook, just the tabula rasa of a clueless 20-year-old. Nonetheless, for a moment, I was mesmerized like Dante seeing Beatrice for the first time or James Joyce seeing his future wife!

The Otherness of Rome

Rome **didn't come** across **as a complete surprise** to me at first. I came to her with a B.A. in philosophy, eight years of Latin, and a treasure trove of trivia as a cradle of Roman Catholicism, etc. It was the day-to-day life of the city that was new, e.g. the clothing was more subdued. Romans mix their wine with mineral water; their bars were bright and mirrored; **people spoke Italian**; the Colosseum was not tilted (like that tower in Pisa); the Trevi Fountain was a pool; their pizzas were better than ours; their food was less processed and less refrigerated; some hospitals had mining buckets instead of elevators with doors; some buildings had squat toilets at floor level that could build up your calves if you could keep your balance; there were siestas during the work day; Italian TV was terrible except for the commercials which were well crafted and suspenseful - they never told you what the product was until the very end of the commercial. In Italy, there was even a **lottery to choose which songs** and versions **would make the top ten charts** that year based on publishing the lyrics and artists' names in advance. Later, the songs put to music would be televised at the **San Remo Festival** and the winners were proclaimed.

A personal observation, I discovered that when we, as foreigners, witnessed the drama of a kid pitching a fit in Italian, we tended to view it dispassionately. Language filtered the pathos and the child came across as cute, i.e., **less irksome and disagreeable than** if he acted out **in English**. (Unless, of course, he is your step son, Guido Cantalupi – Guido the Bawler - in which case you give him a piece of your mind)

Given time, I could cite a list of other Roman believe-it-or-nots practices that you won't find mentioned in Rick Steves' travel guides.

Rome was more than I hoped for! An alternate title for this book was 'Visitations.' But as with Mary's visitation by Gabriel, it wasn't the case that I visited the Eternal City. No! **The city came knocking on my door** with her food, her people, her customs, and Godly tidings aptly described by Emily Dickinson in this poem:

"There came a day at Summer's full,

Entirely for **me**.

I thought that such were for the Saints-

Where Resurrections be-"

Emily has a way of keeping us by her side when life comes calling (with visitations) e.g. whether the occasion is **a wake** as in:

"There's something quieter than sleep

Within this inner room

It wears a sprig upon its breast and will not tell its name."

Or while watching **a hummingbird**:

"Within my Garden rides a Bird

Upon a single-wheel

Whose spokes a dizzy music make

As 'twere a traveling mill"

We feel privileged to share such moments with her through poetry. In like vein, I hope to bring you along with me, especially all of you who have never lived in a foreign country yourself, and ask you not to examine my reporting with a jeweler's loupe **but virtually** as fellow travelers exploring an alien world and assuming the role of "ignorance abroad," to paraphrase Mark Twain.

The Thrill of Going native

For example, one cultural quirk that I observed in the Italian character and used to my advantage was **"La bella figura,"** which translates to **"saving face."** It came in handy when a classmate, "Tragedy Jack," who never really mastered Italian, received some money from home during our second year overseas and he asked me to take him to a good restaurant for real (not college) food. And if I would interpret, he would pay for my meal. Deal!

The restaurant I chose for our night in the town **served** a brand of wine (a moselle) that I really liked, called, **"Est! Est! Est!"** It got that name from a legend about an itinerant friar in the Middle Ages who customarily sent his squire ahead every evening to find an inn with good wine. If he found one he would write, "Est" (it is) on the shingle outside and they would dine and spend the night. Well, the squire hit the jackpot with an unbelievable find i.e. a moselle-like wine and he marked the spot "Est! Est! Est!" They both drank themselves to paradise.

Well, Jack and I got a table. I ordered wine, veal milanese and canelone. Jack went with wine, carbonara, and a veal dish he heard about but never tried called osso buco. My meal was great but Jack didn't like his veal. **"Send it back,"** he said. **"It tastes funny."** When the bill came he paid for everything but the meat dish. The waiter balked, and the other diners perked up and stared at us ugly Americans. The waiter grabbed the plate and disappeared through the swinging doors to have the chef taste it. Meanwhile, I was sitting at arm's reach of a basket of rolls and I noticed a big juicy fly on the wall, so I grabbed the roll, squished the fly, and returned the bread to the basket.

Within minutes, the waiter returned with Jack's plate, plopped it on the table, and announced to us and the onlookers, "This meat is fresh."

"Fresh? Fresh?" I shouted, "I'll show you fresh!" And I picked up the roll and displayed the bloody fly on the bottom for all to see. I received unanticipated applause from the other diners. To save face, our red-faced waiter returned the plate to the kitchen, then brought the meat back wrapped in a package and said, "Take this and bring it to the police. If they say it's fresh, come back and pay your bill."

"We agreed and left with the "dinner- to-go." Jack was about to throw it in the trash but I shouted, "Wait. Give it to me. I'll eat it tonight." Let me tell you, even on a full stomach, "La bella figura" lightly sauced hit the spot and made me think, "Wow! I might get to like this country, after all!"

A few weeks later, my mother came to Rome to visit. My sister had just gotten her first teaching position which came with the perk of a master card (very unusual for women to obtain in those days), and used it to pay for mom's trip. Mom and I ate without incident at the same restaurant where Jack and I had dined and afterward, we strolled down the Via Veneto. Unfortunately, when we passed a local beauty, mom caught me in the act of fluoroscoping the lady, and objected,

"Have you grown an owl's neck under your Roman collar, Butch?"

"All part of socialization, Connie," I told her. "Just being appreciative."

Nevertheless, my mother's remark raised an interesting question. "Had my stay in Italy exiled my conservative German and Irish genes to the genetic Limbo thereby remaking me 100% Italian? Mamma Mia! Saints preserve us! I'd rue the day on which I'd have to swill **Grappa (Italian brandy)** to stave off the DTs at some future date instead of good 'ole Johnny Walker. Have you ever tasted grappa? TERRIBLE!

P.S. I always wore a simple Roman collar in public. Our protestant brethren sported high stiff 360° around collars which we called, "hickey hiders" as befitting their married status. Inexplicably, it was **also** our Rector's surname.

****

My Infamous Article (Left Brain)
(1968)

At the end of my first year in Rome, a boon/bane opportunity came my way in the form of a student journal where 1st-year theologians could safely express their ideas without faculty censorship (or so we thought). When I say faculty, I'm speaking of our handlers at the residence, not the Greg professors. They believed that we were incapable of producing anything of substance that could cause controversy but they hadn't banked on me. My motto - once suppressed, twice as bold and so I wrote a beautiful piece called **"Symbolic Sinning"** which dealt with the moral weight and value of ethical decisions taken by persons in transitions, such as when moving through cultural changes, personal crises, or developmental stages. **Someone tipped the faculty off**, probably an envious classmate, urging them to read the galleys and stop the publication of my article. They probably thought it promoted "situation ethics" which I was not advocating. My sources were Fuchs' "Fundamental Option" and St. Augustine's observation in the CITY of GOD, (those dummies!). They returned my manuscript to me loaded with insults and marginalia and **sent me to Professor Fuchs to complete my humiliation.** Fuchs was the preeminent professor of Moral Theology in the Catholic pantheon and my professor. **He had suffered censor himself** from Pius VI for being in favor of birth control and voting yes on the commission charged with studying the issue by John XIII. Fuchs didn't decide the birth control controversy by cold reason alone. He consulted the conscience of faithful Catholics who practiced birth control and consulted the Holy Spirit in their decision-making process. The Vatican frequently spied upon him and when they visited his lectures, he protected himself by changing gears and reciting a list of bibliographies in place of the lecture.

Fuchs knew all the Vatican spies by name because Italians love titles and if you are a professional spy you would want everybody to know it or what's the use. Only Frenchmen spy incognito.

I made my way obediently to the University and entered Fuchs' study with my tail between my legs and head lowered. Fuchs sat me down and began with a disclaimer. i.e. that the criticisms scribbled across my pages belonged to my faculty and not to him.

"Are these your ideas?" he asked.

"Yes, professor," I answered.

"I see you quote Charles Curran in your article. Don't do that. He's just a popularizer of my ideas." (Fr Charles Curran was a famous moral theologian at Catholic University in Washington, D.C.) **Fuchs continued, "I shared your article** with some professors **in the philosophy department**. ('Oh, oh, the philosophy again,' I thought). **And they were impressed," said Fuchs**

"At first," he continued, "I thought the title 'Symbolic Sinning' was not the right word. Then I thought they were the only words. With your permission, I would like to use some of these ideas in a lecture."

'What!'

"The article needs deepening but it's good."

"You mean I should publish it?"

"If you believe in it, why not? But don't quote Charles Curran. He's not original. This article is."

I was dumbfounded. I thanked him, returned to the faculty jackals, and announced, **"Fuchs says publish it."** And they did. Part of my genius was that I was unschooled. I didn't know a lot of theology. But I knew about the fundamental option and I read St. Augustine's "City of God." I wasn't quite a scholar but I was a thinker and sometimes an unfettered and untrained thinker **gets it.**

I take on a professor from the Gregorian UNIV (1969)

On one occasion, **Professor Borassa** consented to lecture at our college in English. Professor Borassa was a published expert on Trinitarian Theology. I confess I hadn't been attending his Latin lectures at the Greg nor had I read his book, so I listened attentively to see if that was worthwhile doing so. All went smoothly until he claimed that the Trinity was an absolute mystery that would never have been known had it not been revealed and that it challenged and frustrated thinkers for millennia and mainly served as a matrix for more accessible mysteries such as Salvation, Creation, and Sanctification. It was absolutely outside of human experience.

I raised my hand and said, "Professor, I agree that the Trinity had to be revealed to be known but I am not sure that once revealed it remains outside of human experience. Certainly, for the man Jesus, it was an existential and knowable truth and throughout time many trinitarian worshipers experience their God as Trinitarian." Today, I could have added that Baltasar holds that the light of faith aligns us on a modest level with the experience of Christ enjoyed in his human nature of "his Father and of himself in the Holy Spirit" (Keys, Aldan Nichols Pg.30) **See, I was right! Hurray, I was doing theology!**

Professor Borassa conceded my point and added that the great Karl Rahner was presently working on a more existential treatment of the Trinity. I returned to my chair, validated that my insight was cutting edge, and hated by conservative colleagues who had read Borrassa's book and attended his lectures in vain. It amazed me how few of them were capable of processing new information critically. I remember them pretending to be liberal thinkers, laughing when St. Christopher was removed from the list of saints. How they mocked traditional Catholics as suckers, saying, "Now all those useless statues will have to be removed from the dashboards of millions of cars. Ha Ha Ha."

I said, "You understand, gentlemen, that canonizations are reputed to be infallible declarations of the Church. So, how do you reconcile this decision with that tradition?" I asked, "Please, share your scholarly wisdom and amaze me!"

No response! Score one for us gadflies! And so, I left these snobs licking their wounds as they returned to the land of Nodding Off. **Sweet dreams, America's best**!

Update Feb 20, 2022:

Today, I read Aidad Nichols' book on Balthasar and found some of the very ideas I shared that day with Prof. Borassa back in 1968, i.e., Balthasar also teaches that as human beings, we too can commune with and experience the Triune Godhead of whom Jesus spoke. "By grace and worship **our mortal senses** and imagination **are** disciplined and **re-shaped** pneumatically through the working of the Holy Spirit." ("Key to Balthasar" pg,30) Human existence is not just attuned to God as an **Absolute Being** (a Philosophical concept of Karl Rahner) but as a **Trinitarian Being**, understood in interpersonal terms. Balthasar taught that God revealed Himself as a dynamic relationship of persons, the doctrine of the Holy Trinity. And so, if one says "yes" to God's Glory, i.e. His transcendental beauty as it shines and beguiles us in the world and especially in the Christ form, we can simultaneously honor Him as the source of the transcendence beckoning, calling out to us in the concrete forms we see. (Key to Balthasar p.67) **'Doxa'logy.**

****

New Ideas and New Skills — but no brass ring

Over the years, some great ideas came my way, although they usually arrived a shade too late for me to be credited as their author. For example, I once preached a sermon in the USA entitled **"The Murder Trial of Jack in the Beanstalk."** or how Jack went from thief to assassin in a single swing of an ax. It was part of a Bible study week aimed at encouraging the congregation to bring their adult minds to those same biblical texts that they read as children and curb their expectations for "Happily ever afters" in this life. Guess what happened? Two weeks later, **my fractured fairytale** appeared on national TV in an acclaimed two-part series. If I ever find that mole in my congregation who leaked it, he'd be lucky to get off with fifty rosaries when leaving my confessional (spawn of Satan!) Then again, it's hard for me to imagine hordes of opportunists **finding original material to plagiarize in most church productions**. So, I suppose, there's really no cause for alarm. I did put on an excellent Exodus play called "Thou shalt not covet thy neighbor's Tombs" (very well- received.)

At a future date, I plan to produce "The Cartel of Five Oil-Rich Virgins" to get some skin in the media game like my brother did. As you recall, he did a documentary on the Discovery Channel on the <u>Shroud of Turin</u>. Wait a minute, brother. That's religion? That is supposed to be my bag. Stay on **your own side** of the easel, Ray! (OK. Maybe I'm jealous.)

C.f. Body and Bible by Bjom Krondorfer for a scholarly Treatment of Bibliodrama.

Differentiating Schools of Thought
Theological debates are commonplace. (a preview)

The contrast of theology from above vs. theology from below (Some Heavy Stuff)

The socio-biologist E.O. Wilson aspired to become an ornithologist as a child. Fate had other plans. He **lost an eye** at age seven (from a fishing accident) and **suffered hearing** loss as a teenager. Without binocular vision and acute hearing, a career in ornithology was out of the question. Downcast, but still a hard-wired naturalist, he looked about, and there at his feet lay another species that deserved studying – **ant colonies,** which required only one good eye and reasonable hearing to decipher its secrets and fill any naturalist with a life-time of joy. He became a world-class entomologist but after specializing in one social insect, Prof. Wilson then turned **an** eye to socio-biology, then biodiversity, and finally, you guessed it, 'Ant-thropology.'

Balthasar began his life like E.O. Wilson with both eyes trained on the peaks of German high culture and the promise of a career as a concert pianist. Then fate found him at a Jesuit retreat. Fate (by another name) was working overtime it seems by making him a great theologian. 'Fr. Henri de Lubac' called Balthasar the most cultured man in Europe. **Like E.O. Wilson, Balthasar became a one-of-a-kind thinker** with a **mission** to refurbish Catholic tradition which had grown dry and abstract and needed pruning to flourish again. While previous theologians such as St. Augustine seem earthbound in finding apt metaphors for the sacred, Augustine used human psychology as an analogy to understand the Trinity, a theology "from below." Balthasar courageously started with dogmatic paradigms e.g. the **Trinity as** a metaphor and tool for understanding **Man.** He uses the Trinitarian **dogma** i.e. the processions of the Son from the Father and the spiration of the Holy Spirit from the Father and the Son and then Christ's life **as examples** of what **human love** should be when measured against **Divinity's.** Unabashedly and somewhat uncritically scriptural, Balthasar also drew from the legacy of

Patristic authors, and early ecumenical councils to bless us with a "theology from above."

As a theologian, **Karl Rahner**, his rival, employed a more secular and anthropological point of departure than Balthasar's for elucidating and defending the faith. Rahner enlisted the insights of the atheist Martin Heidegger (Rahner's teacher and himself a product of Jesuit schooling) to erect a 'holy mountain' from the 'anthills' of human thought. Rahner repurposed Heidegger's philosophical **insights concerning** man's 'being in the world' and used these philosophical musings in his first book "Spirit in the World." After that, Rahner raises further questions as to what drives human beings, anchored in this world (Dasein), to desire the 'ever greater,' to undertake this transcendental quest for meaning in which **being irreducible** is implied i.e. being the goal of all human striving. Mankind is Finitude in search of finality, human synapses opening up to **Being** with a capital "B"? This was the context of his companion book "Hearers of the Word."

The Battle of Titans

Since biblical times, through the Patristic, and into the present, there were different currents of theology co-existing in the Church simultaneously. Public debates among scholars with differing opinions were a source of entertainment in the Middle Ages. And so, when a firebrand theologian today like **Balthasa**r (the Champion of art and beauty- right brain) excoriates a colleague, **Karl Rahner,** (the champion of interiority and Thomism- left brain) and gainsay Rahner's claim that God <u>cannot</u> be known <u>objectively</u> in the **image** of Christ but only *non-objectively* as the condition for human self-understanding. (Key p. 36) Par for the course. Balthasar claims that, unlike the Wright Brothers, **Rahne**r's methodology called Transcendental Thomism, remains stuck on the runway of intra-human mental structures and never reaches the **clouds of glory.**

85

<u>Are you confused yet?</u> **Let's go further**

With the gauntlet thrown, Rahner counter-attacks by saying that **Balthasar**'s mythopoetic approach to theology is anachronistic in the post-modern world and if **the church** wishes to survive, it **should uncouple** some **beloved images** and embrace mysticism or it will disappear. I've drawn on both theologians in my religious life and agree with Yogi Berra that when you come to a fork in the road, **choose both**. That's what C.S. Lewis did to resolve <u>this clash</u> of the mythical and anthropological approaches by saying that **in the man, Jesus, "Myth has become Fact" and that's no myth!**

****

Ultimate Fighting words

How can one explain or authenticate Christ's deeds or words? Only Christ's "FORM," says von Balthasar. *Yes let me say it again, Balthasar strongly disagrees with Rahner and discounts his whole metaphysical approach by insisting that the form of Christ found in church tradition doesn't need any of Rahner's philosophical insight into the dynamics of the human mind, 'either to anticipate in advance or retrospect belief. There is no need or structure in man that can explain or authenticate Christ's deeds and words. "Only Christ's Form," says Balthasar, <u>"makes those words and deeds</u> lucidly plain and <u>self-authenticating."</u>

Take a deep breath!

*Readers, I have some good news: The rest of this book won't be this dense. It will include 10% sweat (Thinking), 70% candy (Story), and 20% the follies of this 20-year-old seminarian! So, keeping it in perspective, "Pardonnez -moi ce caprice d'enfant" - pardon my immaturity. (from a song by Mireille Mathieu).

Visitors to our Bell Jar

Three visitors come to a calling

I was haunted like Scrooge by three spirits: past, present, and future

While at NAC

I didn't explore many churches during my stay in Rome. When visitors came to the city, I obliged them with a tour of only three churches - St Peter's in Chains to view the Moses of Michelangelo, Santa Maria Sopra Minerva, a church built upon a pagan temple that houses a famous baroque statue of the Risen Christ, nude except for a golden athletic strap, (we dubbed it the church of the Golden Jock), and, of course, St Peter's Basilica. Art aside, I didn't find empty churches between services very inspirational or transcendental any more than I would be visiting an empty theater. **The only in-church transcendental experience I ever had** (between services) **was in Westminster Abbey** as I stood in the Poet's Corner where my bicameral mind was pleased to see Charles Darwin's Plaque among the poets. By chance, I looked down at the plaque beneath my feet and saw the name **George Frideric Handel**. Do you know how many hours I spent as a teenager listening to his "Water Music" in the parlor of our house eating Oreos, as the summer breezes elbowed the curtains apart with drafts of cool air from our garden? Of course, you don't. How could you? And that's OK. But let me tell you something. The day I realized I was standing on the plaque with Handel's name on it, **I dropped to my knees and wept**. Other London churches held no special charm for me. With so many images of knights in armor on display atop their sarcophagi, the places resembled British war memorials rather than sanctuaries, to tell the truth. That didn't stop me at a later date from purchasing some brass rubbings of those same knights to hang on my study. But back then, those knightly effigies rubbed me the wrong way. I suppose turnabout is fair play as the English say.

Ghost from my childhood

Well, since I was unwilling to go to visit churches, their patrons would have to come to NAC and visit me. I can remember three visitors of note. First, **Bishop Fulton J. Sheen,** was my idol and a family favorite while I was growing up. He had a television show called, "Life Is Worth Living." Such a charismatic speaker. Every season he grew more dramatic and camera-conscious. He became so popular that he actually stole Uncle Miltie's (Milton Berle) audience. Miltie hosted the biggest TV comedy show of the day. On two occasions during my stay in Rome, Bishop Sheen and I passed each other on the college staircase. The first time, he asked me my name and I whimpered timidly.

"And where are you from?" he asked.

"Brooklyn, Bishop."

"Very good!" he nodded.

On our second meeting, he looked at me with cavernous eyes and the gaunt cheeks of a cadaver. (reminiscent of **Zachary** who was the **host of a kid's monster show.**) He spoke my name, then took a few steps, stopped, turned around, and added, "I always meet you on the stairs."

And I responded, with the hackneyed, "Yes, Your Excellency, me going up and you going down."

I swear I said it by reflex as a rejoinder, but it did have an element of truth. Sheen's time had passed. He was unprepared for the liberal ideas of Vatican II and he harped on young priests celebrating **Masses**

<u>Underground</u>. **"You can smell mildew on their robes,"** he quipped. Yeah, and maybe bump into Alice.

On one occasion, I came back to the college well after midnight through the basement and I almost tripped on Bishop Sheen prostrate in prayer in front of one of the altars. I was stealthy and he never noticed my presence but I noticed his sincerity and devotion firsthand. There he was as I always thought of him, the Real McCoy, a saintly man. When I reported this to my friends at lunch, they thought it strange and so I even joked about it so as not to tear up. "I don't think it strange for a man of his age to have a prostrate condition." Nevertheless, as I walked away, I wondered whether Sheen was my spiritual director, would he discount me as one of those risible and superficial **mold-encrusted new priests** he lampooned or deem me as sincere for my age as he was at his. I was very sensitive back then and maybe I still am.

Pope Paul VI visit (1968)
"Haunt me later, Mr. Pope, I'm busy."

Bittersweet as that first visit was, this <u>next visit</u> was simply bitter. **It was announced that Paul VI was coming to visit NAC**. He was the Pope who, ignoring the advice of the "experts" like our Professor Josef Fuchs, **condemned the practice of birth control** threatening that those who use contraceptives would be denied Holy Communion. This decision would land hardest on the poor who could ill-afford more children than they could support. Truth be known, I have no idea why the pope decided to visit us but **I strongly doubt that our nuns would welcome him** back after he gave the college the gift of a lamb which unfortunately enjoyed chasing these saintly women over hill and dale (and remember Rome has seven hills). This was exactly what the donkeys did to my grandma at the Catskill Game Farm, bless her hide. For my part, **I decided to boycott his visit and take up bowling.** I was not a super jock. I didn't dare try out for the soccer team at NAC as Tom did. Nonetheless, I was pretty adept at pitching horseshoes in the Catskills with my grandpa, and tearing up a ping-pong table in our basement, and playing doubles handball after school. So, on the eve of the papal visit, I went down by myself to the bowling alley, a semi-automatic single-lane affair, and turned the power on. There was only one ball in the rack which I picked up, studied, cradled, and launched at the pins, knocking seven down - pretty good. But, suddenly the game was over. **The ball never returned.** I walked down, peered under the hood, and there was my ball, teetering on falling into one of several holes on a ball return wheel that resembled a telephone dial, ready to pick it up and deposit it on a ramp to return to sender. No worries. All I would have to do is to slide backward under the hood and kick the ball into the hole - which I did. And then all hell broke out. The cleaning bar came down and moved forward to sweep me and the fallen pins to the rear. I had to swim over it, then flip on my back to avoid its return. Then, the action was passed to its tag-team partner, the pin setter who, armed with a fistful of pins attempted to crush me like the hammers of a 'Whack-A-Mole' and leave me limp, lifeless, and tenderized while the prodigal ball rolled slowly back to start. <u>Call me shallow</u> but the only thought I had during the ordeal was, "<u>Will this machine label me as a strike or a spare?</u>" I'm not kidding! Needless to say, I escaped the melee, bruised, bleeding, and shaken. I decided to go back to ping pong or any sport that didn't involve heavy machinery.

Spirit from the Future (1969)

During my second year of study, a **young lady from Hawaii** appeared at the college. She was black, beautiful shapely, racially diverse (African and Asian), and given that there was no seminarian from her state, I was chosen to escort her around Rome. This wasn't your usual matronly visitor with blue hair or a harrowed mom with 11 kids. This was a trophy visitor capable of raising the eyebrows of my conservative brethren, who in our all-white seminary wouldn't assume she was a relative of mine. **She wore** a delightfully scandalous **short dress as I recall (very well).**

Dutifully, I donned my Roman collar, she took my arm and we began the tour judiciously focusing on outdoor monuments like the Colosseum and Roman Forum. However, when we passed St. Peter's, she said, "I want to go inside."

"Impossible," I said, "With a short dress and bare shoulders, they won't allow us in."

"They'll let me in," she assured me.

"I'm talking about **you**," I said. "I'm not the one with a short skirt and bare shoulders!"

"Let's try," she said and we walked up the steps only to be stopped by a Swiss Guard who drew his sword and indicated where her dress should end.

"Unzip me," she said. I did without asking why as she lowered the dress to the proper length, held it to her chest, looked directly at the stunned Swiss Guard with sword unsheathed and dangling in defeat and we strolled inside. I was in shock! I could hardly catch my breath as I quickly zipped her up. Even a semi-iconoclast like me had his limits. We didn't stay long but it made me think, this building wasn't a church to her or many other foreign tourists. It was a museum. Maybe just posting some rules of decorum and a dress code outside would be better than enforcing them at sword point. **Or why not just let the art inside speak and be done**?

N.B. **An office of information was developed** and staffed by seminarians in **1971** which bore the brunt of indignation from **women,** young and not so young, who had been turned **away from St. Peter's because of their outfits**. "Sometimes, we let them use our bathroom to adjust their skirts to a suitable length if this were in the realm of possibility or we would leave a few husbands waiting (in the bathroom) in their skivvies while their wives toured the Basilica in their husbands' pants." (Aggiornamento pg.344) What was considered bizarre behavior on my part and that of my Hawaiian guest, actually became Vatican policy after I left. Sic manet la comedia divina.

Allow me to leave my guest from Hawaii and my narration about visitors to share something personal. As much as I enjoyed showing people around Rome as a student, suggesting what to see, where to purchase souvenirs, and where to eat well and reasonably (unless they invited me to dine, which prompted me to recommend pricier venues), **I never thought my service as a guide ever reached the level of evangelization**. Yes, the tours elicited some pride and appreciation of church history, but did they foster introspection or deepen the faith of these tourists, I wondered? Powerful, yes, transformative, maybe. As Balthasar says, maybe beauty is a divine message in itself. Yet, many visitors exit the lampblack dome of the planetarium in New York, after seeing the wonders of the universe and then switch gears in the naked light of day, and wonder - "Where did I park my darn car?" Can I cite Gustov Mahler as a case in point?

****

The Evanescence of ART

In 1905 Gustov Mahler wrote a song cycle called, "The Youth's Magic Horn." One of the twelve songs was dedicated to the legend of St. Anthony's preaching to the fishes. As the story goes, Anthony came to preach in a church but no one showed up, so he went to the river and preached to the fish. They jumped up, splashed, and enjoyed the sermon. But, when it was over, they hadn't changed. The pikes remained thieves, the carps glutton, the crab crawled backward and all remained the same as before. People loved Mahler's piece but at the evening's end, they exited the concert without their programs to hail a cab and get on with their lives

Today I am **less skeptical** about art's staying power **after reading Gadamer** who links art appreciation to philosophy (ontology) and **Balthasar** who crafted a theology of beauty. Art can even serve as an intermediary object (psychology) between us and the void, states Psychiatrist, Wilford Bion of Tavistock. That's why people kiss icons, build shrines, carve statues, and celebrate holidays namely - to make the unseen present, through art's sacramental touch. That's why the 4th-century bronze statue of St. Peter has the toes worn off from the touches and the kisses of the faithful who have visited St. Peter's Basilica for over seven centuries and probably why they put athletic support on the nude Resurrection statue of Christ in the church of **Santa Maria Sobre Minerve** i.e. to prevent the faithful from using certain parts of the statue as a talisman for future fertility. Personally, I believe that Renaissance statues portraying eternal truths should eschew such puritanical considerations under the rubric of ars gratia artis. (Consider how 'Pieta' breaks the rules of proportionality in favor of depicting Mary's state of mind: She's a mighty big mother by human standards and maybe that's the point.) How many times in the news have I seen the "pieta" replicated by war victims carrying their dead from the battleground?

If I only knew back then that there was a theology of beauty

I also wish I had as a tour guide known about **Hans Urs von Balthasar** when I studied in Rome. He was a theologian who had a background as a classical pianist and a doctorate in German Studies. As a result, he produced a narrative theology that emphasizes beauty as one of the qualities of being, a transcendental quality of God, standing toe to toe with truth and goodness. His powerful writing can ferry the reader down to hell with Jesus on Good Friday and up with Dante to Paradise Regained at Easter. That happened to me once I read **Balthasar**. He **would have made my guided tours more evangelical** and my studies more holistic and allowed me to view religious art not only didactically but as existential vehicles of Divine glory. We desperately need such creative minds since familiarity tends to blunt the senses from finding God and enjoying His creation as His creation. Familiarity can fiendishly erase those jokes that we once knew by heart, or, more to the point, cause us to give works of art only a passing glance or a rare visit. It isn't because art and humor are evanescent by nature. It's because the speed of darkness is faster than the speed of light in this fallen world of ours. - where our mind can only host a fistful of ideas at a time. (fact)

*****

Adventures
Learning Mission In Sito

Caminar con aquel campesino

Los dos recorriendo el mismo camino

Hablando de uno,hablando de vino

Contando los sueños y como vivimos

While walking along I met up with a fellow

Along the same path that I decided to follow

We spoke of ourselves; we spoke about wine

He shared me his dreams and I gifted him mine

(from the song "For Example "by Nicola di Bari)

My sister, Margie, told me a joke. I don't know its origin but it says a lot about my own presumptions, filters, and blind spots that shaped my initial encounter with Roman life.

It goes like this: On the opening night of a deluxe theater on the West Coast, the usher on his rounds comes upon a man sprawled across three seats.

"You can't occupy all these seats, sir. Choose one and sit up straight."

There was no response.

"Alright, I'll get the manager!" The manager came and read him the riot act. Still, the man didn't budge.

"Okay," said the manager, "I'm calling the cops." The policeman came with a citation book, stood over the man and asked, "What is your name?"

The man moaned, "Ralph."

"And where are you from?"

The man pointed and said, "The balcony, sir. I fell from the balcony."

The Zen of Motorcycle Maintenance
(before the book with a similar title came out)

I didn't arrive in Rome by helicopter or balcony but I did come without wheels. After two years, my family gifted me a Lambretta motor scooter. Before that, my introduction to motorized transportation was a kamikaze misadventure **on a small motorcycle, 200cc** down a hill alongside the Vatican wall. I hadn't ridden even a motorbike before, let alone a motorcycle, but my friend, 'Tragedy Jack' had an old one stowed away and he assured me, "There's nothing to it." He showed me the accelerator, the brakes, and how to start the engine. What he didn't show me was the **'kill' switch** which I needed as the brakes failed and I careened faster and faster down the hill to my doom. Out of desperation, I veered the cycle into the drain gulley and then into the wall where protruding bricks splayed my fingers in a thousand directions. Needless to say, ownership of such vehicles was explicitly forbidden by our college bylaws (for safety reasons), so I couldn't report my accident to the college infirmary. I had no choice but to straighten and reset my own fingers, leaving me unable to play Flight of the Bumblebee on piano happily ever after. (I hate that piece) Unfortunately, it **did** mess with my billiard stroke. Schade!

Jack took charge of the cycle and snuck it back to the college. It's hard to believe this happened **to me**, the son of a police lieutenant at a **motorcycle precinct** in Brooklyn. I guess that my belated father must have pulled some strings in heaven to prevent me from becoming a better **biker** and catching up with that **nun on the Vespa, the one with the mirror-sunglasses.** Thanks, dad. I guess owe you! Schade!

My friend Jack was a large freckled Irishman, that is to say, a large Irishman with freckles, and an accomplished if haphazardly prone athlete (with the emphasis on hazard), who spent his days chuckling his way serendipitously from disaster to disaster. I don't know where he lives today, but if he is still alive, and this being summertime here, **I'm sure he is being wheeled into an ER at this very moment** with acute barbecue-related injuries like, singed hair and a pair of molten sunglasses soldered to his face. In his teens, **his mother burned his hair off with a sparkler on the Fourth of July**. When I met him in his twenties, this pattern of misfortunes continued. He managed to break no less than 7 pairs of sunglasses in a season, the last of which he destroyed by tossing a dictionary on them in a drawer. My only hope is that he is never allowed to be around fissionable material and never gets married. Because of his history, I dubbed him 'Tragedy Jack' with affection, and the title stuck. He reciprocated by labeling me, 'The Vatican's own Evil Knievel.' Eventually, I got a Skooter and finally a car. I hope that he is on the mend from his latest misadventure and may he live haplessly ever after. .

****

Hitching Rides

I really didn't need wheels for my first two years overseas. Hitchhiking in Europe at the time was a perfectly respectable mode of transportation, and my first attempt at thumbing a ride was well received by a young German driver itching to interview a beatnik (me) and learn about the hippy movement. Before I left the States, I should have packed myself a stick-on goatee, a turtleneck sweater, and a set of bongos, to earn greater acceptance by European students. "Schade." Oh well, too late now. By the way, <u>Schade</u> is a word I picked up in Deutschland meaning too bad or what a pity and I use it now regularly to replace a vulgar American word that begins with "S."

As I got into his car, I could smell notes of beer in the air. Next, he pulled out his trumpet and played as we drove. He pumped me about **my** favorite jazz artist and I turned the question back to him out of politeness and ignorance. I must say though, that to my virgin ears, this guy sounded pretty accomplished on that horn. It was very loud. His Jezebel produced such screechingdecibels that I begged him to let me sit in the back seat and he did. He took me home, invited me to dinner, and asked volumes about the beat poets and Bob Dylan. I relaxed and found myself on more familiar ground. He asked me (in passing) what I did and when I told him I was studying for the priesthood, he inquired how I saw the mission of the church. **I decided to quote the beat poet Ferlinghetti and said that the church was like a lighthouse nightly moving its megaphone over the seas of the world.** He said, "What does that mean?" and I said, "I don't quite know. but as a beatnik, Ferlinghetti might have been on pot at the time." We laughed – while my countrymen were smoking weed, I was doing fine on altar wine. Though I never went to Woodstock, I did have some exposure to the beat poets via WQXR classical radio and yearly visits to the open-air art shows and the book stalls in Greenwich Village (a beatnik stronghold.) Good enough. My host was too buzzed to know the difference between me and a real beatnik. The next morning, I was served a hearty breakfast. He asked me, "Wo willst du **hingehen,**" and I said, "**Die Autobahn**." So, he drove me back to the highway to hitch again.

I hitchhiked my way to Frankfurt. There I noticed thousands of political slogans and graffiti splashed across the University walls. From there, I made my way across town to a students' watering hole and was kindly invited to spend the night with them in one of the dorms. In their common room was a bearded guy with a cello. I asked if he could play me a waltz by Strauss. "Strauss? Bourgeois hack! I'll play some real music," and he segued into a Bach partita. Darn! Even the music in this country was politicized. Paul Simon was right when he wrote "The words of the prophet are written on the subway walls." Evidently, that is also true of University walls and sheet music. One of the other students asked me what I studied and when. I told him, he said his father was a church deacon but he wasn't religious anymore.

"What are you now?" I asked.

"A Marxist," he said.

I didn't know where to go with that, so I pivoted and asked, "Do you play an instrument also?"

"I used to," he said, "The clarinet. But I sold it in Amsterdam for two hits of smack."

"So, you went from religion, the "opiate of the people," to the real thing in Amsterdam?"

"Yes," he said, "I prefer my opium in vapor form." At least he was honest. I found the German students to be by and large more politically sophisticated, and more self-aware on average than Americans, myself included.

The following morning, I left Frankfurt and a few roads thereafter, I came upon **two young ladies from Canada.** They were apparently seasoned travelers judging from their backpacks and a two-seater-portable kayak. I was a little out of breath having just outrun a bull across an open field earlier that day. I hadn't taken notice of him at first, but when I finally saw those massive shoulders, the lowered head, and pawing his legs rehearsing a charge, I did a Buster Keaton toward the nearest stretch of fence, launched my luggage over and followed suit, and pants and underwear to safety. What a relief to be alive and find myself on the opposite side of Fernando in the pleasant company of **travel companions** from Canada to share Germany with. Best of all, they had an extra sleeping bag. We talked and swapped background stories until the cows (and bulls) came home. We spent the night sleeping in an open field, a few miles and a fence away from **the minotaur**. Wow! A bullfight and a sleep-over with two women all in 24 hours. What would my mother say? xxxxx!

Thank God I wouldn't have to outrun a bull again until the following year in Pamplona, Spain. But there I could count on the support of fellow idiots and the anesthetic and antiseptic benefits of a wineskin if my luck or legs gave out. I was beginning to feel like a normal person out in the big and sometimes dangerous world learning how to navigate the every day like lay people with no institutional support. I become the abbot of my inner friary. This was an essential part of my formation apart from academics, and my practicum **in the field**. When I woke the following morning sandwiched between two golden-haired seraphims, I heard the ringing of church bells. Looking at my sleeping companions, I felt a little guilty about not being in church on Sunday. When they awoke, I suggested finding a church and they just laughed. This was a bellwether moment for me. Officially, I was in Rome studying to become a secular priest, a priest in the world not a monk in a monastery. To be successful, I'd have **to strike a balance**. Part of the learning curve in any profession involves taking measured risks. Later, as a therapist, I would notice the qualitative difference between seasoned therapists who underwent therapy themselves and the untried counselors straight out of school who were satisfied with inkblots, lectures, and books. And so, I let Sunday be Sunday, and the three of us continued together on our journey. We finally reached London, our common destination. I was a little winded. (I had just outrun a bull days before.) The ladies stashed their kayak at the train station and we visited the **Tate Gallery** before parting ways. I remember standing between them looking at a large Van Dyke painting which **they asked me to interpret**. I couldn't think of anything profound to say at the moment, but I noticed that the men in the painting were painted in profile to foreshorten their generous noses (detail) and sported flawless goatees. "Look at that beard work," I marveled. "Have you ever seen the like? Now I draw beards on faces in magazines and posters, but I could never match this Van Dyke fellow." Some English folk nearby chuckled which I construed as friendly and we continued to tour the gallery. This time, I fixed on the receding hairline evident in portraits of medieval women "What's your take on this, ladies? Would you guess that medieval artists consider high foreheads (Alopecia) a Bane or a Boon, a cosmetic flaw, or an embellishment like plucked eyebrows? What say ye?" On that note, the local admirers left my lecture in disgust and I mumbled after them, "How like the English to <u>TURNER a</u> blind eye to details and squint at clues that can lead one from chaos to legibility. Is there no trace of Sherlock Holmes left in your souls, sirs, no sleuth bent on finding the truth, solving the riddle?"

It reminded me of the time I asked the German tour guide in Bavaria why there were miniature cannons in the castle's armory. "Oh, they're just salesman's samples," she replied. "Ah," I said, "So, they're not working models designed to take down the enemy's children, the so-called <u>Infantry</u>. (Hermeneutics notices puzzles and learns by asking questions.)

After fish and chips, my friends and I said our goodbyes. "Good luck with your boat ride down the Thames," I waved. (If only their kayak seated three. But I had **vows** to keep and miles to go and dudes to meet, and miles to go and dukes to meet).

The great thing about hitchhiking through Europe is getting to see people both up close and, in their element, a series of stop-action takeaways like museum dioramas. One comes away with mixed feelings of immediacy and detachment, of being there yet not really part of the scene, which proved to be both exhilarating and daring for a guy like me who never had a real and unchaperoned adventure before. These were images both strange and wonderful to frame in memory, and draw upon at my leisure, and maybe exaggerate a little in the telling. I was still a tourist, far from being a seasoned traveler but wise enough to realize that philosophy and theology **detached from lived experience** is simply a game of solitaire or a plate of refried beans. **Real life takes place in person and real Christianity is actualized through living. (too preachy?)**

*****

Language Games

People don't think grass be wet in the morning, but it do– South Carolina wisdom.

"What cannot be said, should not be said." – Wittgenstein.

Finding the right words
1967

Except for a mandated month dedicated to study the first summer, we North American College students were globetrotters, free to choose our summertime destinations, traveling companions, and mode and class of transport, (which was basically whatever our parents could afford).

At the end of the academic year, we were obliged to dedicate a month to study, I chose to go to Perugia, the capital of Umbria, not for its Etruscan Treasure, not for the art of Perugino but to train my tongue to navigate Italian "R's" and savor Perugino chocolates. **I met an American lady** and her son there **in Italian class** and we kept in touch. **She came to my ordination claiming to be my work wife**. My mother, **warden of my virginity**, was not amused. She was even less amused watching us dancing cheek to cheek and completely irate when she watched Diana and I share a custard (Flanning) using the same **spoon.** I can hear her mental ruminations grinding away, "First dancing and now spooning. What next?" No worries, mom. By then, Diana was engaged to an engineer and out of circulation. We were just friends. As a matter of fact, she was my first adult female friend outside the family circle and this paved the way for Sister C.

Words about words
1967

After that month of Italian lessons in Perugia, I still wasn't proficient. But it was time to go on vacation before classes started again. Winter was turning the corner. Once back in Rome, I arrived at the college late one night, well past curfew and I found myself locked out. What to do? I had the flu and was too weak to scale the wall so I decided to check into a small pensione (hotel) run by nuns. **I was coughing and hacking** and needed some hot tea if I hoped to sleep that night so I drafted a note in my best Italian saying, "I need tea." "I must have tea." "I can't sleep without tea."

Problem, I left out the indefinite article, "de te" (some tea) which made my missive read, "I want you, I need you, I can't sleep without you." The nun gave me a look, handed me the key, and disappeared, confused and a little teed-off. I shrugged and went to bed. The next day, I showed my note to an upperclassman who pointed out the grammatical gaffe.

1970

Another linguist gaffe happened a year later which involved my classmate, Jim T., and one of the Spanish nuns, Maria Concepcion (better known as Miss Conception). They were supervising kids on a parish trip to the beach. Jim came back to NAC really happy.

"Concepcion loves me," he said.

"You're nuts. What makes you think that?"

"She kept handing me sandwiches and admiring my bod and saying, 'What a man' in Spanish."

That didn't sound right. Then it finally dawned on me.

"Jim, she didn't say, 'Que hombre' - What a man. She said, 'Que hambre' - What an appetite. Ha, ha, ha. You ate all her finger food." Well, at least one of his passions was serviced that day.

Pardon my dictionary
1968-71

One of our biggest language problems endemic to our mission outreach in the ghetto was cursing. We had established an after-school for kids of Trastevere and as a result, their school grades rose but their cursing remained pretty much the same. To address this, we made a list of swear words and distributed it to new seminarians working with these kids so they could know when they were being insulted. However, when I became a deacon, I was invited to give sermons in the Nun's Chapel. I didn't realize that I had written my homily on the back of pages from my dictionary of curses. The nuns in the first pews got an eyeful. If attention is any measure, that was the most engaging homily I ever delivered. On the other hand, shame on those ladies for knowing what those words meant! (or at least most of them).

Best Vacations

Venice (1967)

After my Italian lessons in Perugia, having mastered the "R's" well enough to say "Porca la miseria" as easily as rolling cannelloni. I met up with my two traveling companions and we set out for Venice by train. **Mark Twain said**, "There is no surer way **to find out whether you like people** or hate them than to **travel with them**." True that!

One of my companions was a New Yorker Ken from Queens and the other was Will who was a good-looking farm fresh and range-free fellow from Wisconsin. I will not describe him any further out of jealousy. It was he who the girl in the haberdashery aimed at when she tried on a stetson and pretended to shoot him with her hand. Ken was an awkward German-Irish fellow who we dubbed "gyro-gearloose." He was tall, sarcastic, and clever and sported a "DA" style haircut (short for a duck's backside) and sideburns. But despite his many gifts, he turned out to be the worst travel companion I ever had in my four years abroad (except for my brothers who visited me the following year). The fly in the minestrone took the form of Ken's **new Nikon** camera which hung around his neck **like the ones on American tourists who** hang back for photos and **get impaled by a bull** every year **in Pamplona** when they should have been running for dear life. Now that I mentioned tourists, let me say that–

Over the years in Rome, I've watched tourists from other countries sight-seeing at the Vatican Museum. The Italians from cities north and south of Rome were generally jovial and loud. Coming from settings where art was just as ubiquitous as in Rome, they saw vacation more as a chance to have fun than to be served another scoop of cultural gelato!

After all, what could another locale in the same country offer them that they hadn't seen through local archaeological explorations?

The French tourists were generally playful and well-dressed. They liked to interact with the exhibits with comments, criticisms, witticisms, and cameo shots, forerunners of 'selfie culture.'

The Americans were out and away the fair-haired step-children of tour guides because they were generally clueless, tabulas rasas whom a guide could march past a few choice pieces, make a comment or two, and finally deposit them safe and sound in front of the souvenir stall (which was what they really came for).

"Senore, are these cameos real?"

"Can you show us some holy stuff, maybe a relic for Aunt Maggie? She is very religious and hard to please but she'd never turn her nose up at a papal blessing by John XXIII. Are they still valid?"

Now, the Germans, Ken's ancestors, were without a doubt the most homogeneous group on the spectrum, thoroughly cerebral (except for a couple of Huns). They loved to plant themselves in front of a painting or statue, with their noses in the guidebook, and only after having read every line would they shoot a glance toward the work under consideration. And with a click of the heels and a deep "Sehr Gut," they marched on to the next specimen.

Ken's OCD tendencies made him a lethal camera bug though admittedly he was an excellent editor of our last yearbook in which my infamous article was published. We had barely exited Santa Lucia Terminal in Venice when out came that camera (the first he ever owned) and that joy-killing notebook where he recorded name, place, focal length, aperture, date, shutter speed and God knows what else. Time after time we were left with nothing to do but endure the ritual, as he photographed bridge after bridge after building after vaporetto, after gondola, and so on. When we got back to the college, we were treated to the fruits of his labors. They were terrible, out of focus, over or under-exposed. We told him, "Why don't you just send postcards? You're not even in these pictures and neither is Venice, to be honest." I learned from my interactions from Ken that it is easier to pry your stolen lunch from kodiak beer than to separate a comera bug from his Kodak. Nonetheless, the trip was not a total loss. We did manage to squeeze in an unbelievable night at **the opera at the famous Teatro La Fenice**. Did I mention that one of **my great-granduncles** was a **composer** known for writing popular **Opera Buffa** like 'Corporal Mimi'? In the darkness of the theater, we caught a needed break from Ken's OCD photography, which played on our nerves like a tenor with the hiccups or a flatulating soprano (More so! At least those caesuras are funny in small doses!) Back at the college, we avoided one another for three months then patched things up and became fast friends again but never fellow travelers. Our friendship paid off three years later when our parents flew to Rome for our ordination. On the flight over, Ken's mother was seated next to the mother of my seminary nemesis in America, a guy who tried to talk me out of my scholarship so that he could take my place. Can you believe it? As my mother would say, **"The nerve of some people's children."** I was told that that woman bad-mouthed me non-stop for the whole trip, even though she never met me. Ken's mom never let on that Ken and I were buddies! So, when the plane landed and sons and families reunited, the dirty laundry crawled out with the carry-on luggage provoking some awkward moments, veiled retractions, and a quick getaway on the part of the mother and son combo! And so, as the evening sun retired from the Piazza Navona, Ken, me, and our moms headed for a dinner of pasta and squab at an upscale restaurant while, I imagine, Lady Gossip and her miscreant had to eat crow at some undisclosed location. I'm sure they had "so much" to talk about. No, make that "so many" to talk about!

Yes, friends, her little boy better known as "loving cup" because of his ears had gotten his wish. He was sent to Rome with the rest of us after the Diocese authorized an additional scholarship. What did he gain for all his effrontery? Another four years of living in my shadow. Hurrah!

P.S. **Ken**, my over-starched good friend, **prided himself on cultural sensitivity**, and so, having returned from a missionary summer in Africa in the fourth year, he invited three friends from the African College to have tea in his room. He **decorated** the windows with **wood bark curtains** to make his guests comfortable and to celebrate his trip to their country. But, as they left, Ken felt slighted that they didn't mention the window dressing so he asked one of them.

"Didn't you notice that my curtains are made of bark cloth from your country?"

"Yes, I did."

"Well, what do you think?"

"I think it was a little odd since we **only use** bark cloth to wrap the dead." Lesson. It's hard to strike the right balance between being a missionary and an amateur decorator, though many have died trying. (**The curse of King Tut** stands as a warning **"Thou shalt not covet thy neighbor's tomb."**) **I wonder how his X-mas gifts of inexpensive sundials he purchased from Australia College went over with friends in North America. "Do your homework, Ken! They don't work up north.**

******

To Russia
With luggage (1968)

Isn't tourism supposed to be a low-risk and staged affair, in which we string like rosary beads the mysteries of another country, its tastes, its sights, its smells and relax far from the twisted reach of politics, bills or annoying compatriots (except for the tour guide pitching 'timeshares' and to whom I proclaim, "Sir, I've come to praise Caesar not to buy his house." Pleasure is the reason for holidays abroad. If that's true, my trip to Russia in the late '60s was not a holiday at all. It was a mission, a calculated invasion. In our group of traveling seminarians, we had an investment counselor who swore he could double our disposable dollars on the black market, (he had been to Russia before) and a bookkeeper who by keeping the proper receipts to balance incoming and outgoing capital, hide earned the ill-gotten profits from contraband, which allowed us to buy food, drinks and side trips off the ledgers. We had two seminarian card sharks who kept our state-appointed guide busy while we plied our trade, and my buddy, **Russ** who **spoke Church Slavonic** which was **close** enough **to Russian** so he could eavesdrop and give us the skinny on what was going down. In one part of the tour, we were treated to a night of entertainment in a "typical student cabaret." I still cringe at the memory of a Big Texan tourist with a cowboy hat dancing and hooting on a table next to us. Just made me proud to be an American! (Am I being too snobbish?) Russ, who understood Russian, told us that these young Russian students had never been to a nightclub in their lives. **It was all staged** for the benefit of foreigners like us. We had our games to play. Buried among our 'personal items' were some marketable contraband like hit records, holy cards, bubble gum, stockings, etc. to trade. You should have seen the excitement on the faces of the maids who clean our rooms. Suitcases of treasures to trade for local collectibles. "An Icon for some rock and roll covers anyone?"

"Deal!"

Everything went as expected with two exceptions - the meals and refreshments i.e. breakfast was usually hotdogs and tea which hit my stomach like an alarm clock and menus that falsely advertised entrees their kitchen never featured. As for soft drinks, there was not a Coke to be had. What the soft drink dispenser offered us was a common glass (so bring a clean handkerchief) that you could fill with water for 1 kopek, carbonated water for 2 kopeks, and carbonated water with coloring for 3.

A near catastrophe befell us when Russ (our Church Slavonic speaker) and I went to a cafe to sample the local vodka. Within minutes, three Russians joined our table uninvited, two men and a woman provocatively clad. Russ said he was Ukrainian and I said I was from Czechoslovakia (I used the one sentence I learned in Prague.) They bought it. But when Russ informed me that they were offering us the lady for a night of fun or themselves if we preferred Russ backpedaled, saying, **"No! You guys got us wrong. We're really American tourists."** They were not convinced and started arguing at which point, Russ overturned the table and told me, "RUN!"

"O Bozhe," he cried as we faced the specter of expatriation. Of course, when we rejoined our classmates, we appeared totally macho and downplayed our brush with the gulag. Mission accomplished! The Iron Curtain had been breached and we struck a blow for freedom, free trade, and American 'Know How.' God bless the U.S.A.

While in Russia, Russ told inquisitive Russians that we were theological students and they inevitably asked him what kind of rocks he was looking for. **"We're studying theology, not geology, sirs," he repeated but to no avail.** He should have just said "pitchblende" and left it at that. Maybe Russ' Church-Slavonic was a bit RUSTY or maybe he simply forgot that he was talking theology to atheists.

No trip to Russia would have been complete if it didn't infect the visitor with the pathos of a Dostoevsky novel and I brought back from Moscow my share of tears and political awakenings.

I walk a mile with happiness

She chattered all the way

But left me none the wiser

For all she had to say

I walked a mile with Sorrow

And ne'er a word said she.

But oh, the things I learned from her!

When Sorrow walked with me.

by Robert Browning Hamilton.

That is the difference between a tourist and a humanitarian traveler.

A few days before I joined my friends for our grand tour which
included Moscow, Leningrad, (where another of my great-uncles had
been a conductor of the Czar's orchestra), and Odessa with its beaches
on the Black Sea, and of course, Kiev. I took a side trip alone out of

Moscow, boarding a bus filled with Czech students heading to a famous **monastery in Zagorsk** outside the city. But when we got back, a guy stepped on the bus and told them some bad news. There were cries, wringing of hands, fainting. **"The Russians had invaded Czechoslovakia!** How will we get home?" he sobbed. One woman grabbed me, crying and clinging. I had no words to comfort her. I had just been in their country weeks before, where I met a Czech family on the train. The father was an artist and the mother held their little daughter who was wheezing and coughing incessantly. But despite their problems, they invited me to their house to spend the night and the man and I toured Prague in the morning. The father, who spoke English and French, gave me a phrase to learn, **"I am a Czech Student"** (which nearly got me exiled to Siberia, remember?) When I tried to practice it in their home, my host's little daughter giggled and hid under the covers. In the morning, we toured the Medieval Museum, he showed a statue that his relative had carved on Charles Bridge and after that, we joined some revolutionary activist friends over Stein upon Stein of Pilsner and they discussed their outrage over how **Russia was robbing their country of pitch blend**. This all came back to me on that bus as I witnessed the bitter fruits of Russia's political overreach firsthand in real-time. Until then, I had the privilege of being a-political. History was never my favorite subject. I was classified as 4D - a divinity student, exempt from the draft rolls, while my brothers were sweating the lottery for deployment to Vietnam. Some of the guys at NAC actually left the college to go home and protest the war while I stayed in Rome. I wasn't the only one in a bubble. Sadly, when Gaudium et Spes proclaimed the church's commitment and position in the modern world, few NAC-ers even bothered to read it. Empty boasting, we thought. Maybe if my family ever discussed current events with us or annotated the 'Little World of Don Camillo' with chapters from Das Kapital, I wouldn't have grown up so politically unaware or encased in a church, that was itself a "Little World" within the world. But **naturalized Americans in my parents'**

generation were loath to mention the problems they left behind in Europe nor did they discuss American politics while they basked in the glory of becoming naturalized citizens and patriotic supporters of our role in WWII. World politics was also absent from the curriculum at the Greg until liberation theology forced the issue. Don't applaud! The political theology that was taught at ISEDET in Buenos Aires when I was there (1980-83) was taught by academicians who had no political experience whatsoever.

Yes, I left Moscow in tears and shame. I thought of that family in Prague. Thank God, they were able to emigrate to France, and exhibit their artwork in a show called, 'Circles and Mimes.' And of **the lady who hugged me on the bus,** surprisingly, I saw her picture in <u>Time</u> <u>Magazine</u> months later. She had **been the runner-up to Miss Czechoslovakia the year before**. She escaped to Canada to become a model. I showed Ken the article and quipped, "Blessed are they who comfort, for they shall be comforted." But I kept the tears of political awareness to myself, and only shed them in private – tears for all those poor students on the bus who despaired of ever going home again.

Update: I'm writing this section on February 24, 2022, after hearing an announcer from Odessa reporting the invasion of Ukraine by Russia today. I was unnerved that it came from Odessa which was one of the stops on my Russian tour in 1968. I remember how anachronistic **Odessa** appeared, a replica of bygone beaches in America, like a poor man's version of Palm Beach circa 1940 with change cabanas along the Strand and **a loudspeaker blaring** the Andrew Sisters cover of **"Bei Mir Bist Du Schon."** It could have easily passed as a beach scene in a Fellini film. Today, it came to me as a guilt-laden flashback for having lived a privileged life in a progressive country. Sorry for the interruption. Back to the storytelling.

*****

Vienna
(1969)

The first time I saw her, she was dressed for a ball. The Opera Ring swarmed with people wrapped in 19th-century finery. Horse-drawn carriages shifted out of the way as our tram passed through the gridlock.

The man sitting across from me read my confusion and informed me in English that these folks were extras for the film *Mayerling*, *just cueing up between takes around vats of boiling oil for some gypsy funnel cakes and a cup of gluhwein (hot mulled wine) to fend off Mrs.Holle (winter). Not speaking German, my take away that week was limited: guided tours, food and drink (lecker, lecker), and novel objects.! For example, my little room was barely heated by a tall ceramic stove, so I welcomed the warm offer of a beefy Jung Frau (Not what you think! This "virgin" was a comforter, i.e. a sheet-like sack with a decorated hole in the center to accommodate a feather mattress). When visiting foreign land, travelers like myself enter with an attitude of "surprise me" instead of "where's the Mick D's" and this usually pays off/ but there are some disconcerting times when you could be chased down the block for jay walking or find yourself being frisked at the Opera by an usher who suspect you have a bundt cake under your jacket and yell "Essen ist verboten", then forces you to rent a tie, for the right to stand next to a Hapsburg to listen to an Italian Opera. Ah! Those Hapsburg, really. If my outfit is good enough for the Proms concert in London, it should be acceptable in Vienna. Nah?*

Nonetheless, out and away the best.

Out and away the **best vacation** I had in Europe was years later in the company of the co-authors of this book, Tom Kirshberg, and Jim T. Our destiny, a Xmas winter in Vienna. We checked into the Pension Persky, an older basic pension but spent most of the time out and about in the city for our meals and sightseeing. Tom, who knew some German, always ordered the same, 'A pair of hot dogs.' **There were three other Americans staying there at Persky's, two college freshman women and**

a young sailor on leave who came with his guitar and the need for female company. I passed him serenading the young ladies one evening (wandering minstrel he, ho ho). He asked them if they would like him to perform some early Dylan. I quipped, "Why don't you play the late Pete Seeger?" and I **wasn't** referring to his repertoire.

The six of us met by chance at the state opera house. The offering that evening was 'Madame Butterfly' and when the woman asked me what the opera was about, I said, "It's about a sailor on leave in a foreign country who marries a local, gets her pregnant, and leaves. You know the type." I left them with a wink and a nod. After the opera, Jim, Tom, and I crossed the plaza and went to the Augustina Keller for wine, roast chicken, and maybe two hot dogs.

Then, **the unexpected and unexplainable happened**. At the picnic-style table across the way from ours, three people who might have been at the opera came and took their seats. They were nicely dressed. The very large and sardonic man in a fur-collared coat sat alone on one side and the other two, an elegant lady in an evening dress and a little man whose unbuttoned overcoat revealed a stylish suit and vest with a silver watch chain sat beside her and called the waiter over and ordered peanuts. He looked like a well-groomed Sonny Bono as I recall. When the waiter brought the peanuts, he opened the bag and hoarded them as a prize. The big man across from them was sphinx-like and silent while the lady playfully tried to steal some of the peanuts and Sonny fended her off. He ate them all and ordered a second bag. This time the contest got more intense, hiding, grabbing, and wrestling. What happened next was that the peanut hoarder stood up on the bench, unzipped his fly, inserted the spoils inside, and sat down. Immediately, the large man got on his feet, reached across the table, lifted the little man in the air by the shoulder and **the lady retrieved the bag of peanuts.** This was in a restaurant full of people with a violinist moving among the guests playing Franz Lehár tunes. I thought, "Sie sind verruckt."(they're nuts)

Ich sprache auf Deutsch weil ich in Wien bin. (I'm saying this in German because I'm in Vienna.) But Freud would disagree, "It's merely an example of **transference and peanut envy.**"

Tom couldn't control himself and fell to the floor limp with laughter totally out of commission. Jim dragged him outside to catch his breath. I paid the bill and the three of us followed signs above the underpass to a WC across the street. We shook the snow from our shoes, descended the stairs, and opened up the etched glass door labeled, "pissoir," only to find amidst the urinals and the steam a sketchy man with a banana, who started eyeballing us and then peeling the banana in sync with our zippers, a scene worthy of a panel from Bosch's Garden of Earthly Delights.

Tom convulsed again and needed to be ferried aloft to ground level where he zipped up, tucked in his shirt, and bellowed, "That sick son of ...B" **Are there no public places in Vienna free from perverts?** Not restaurants, not bathrooms, maybe not even museums. Thank God, we left the opera tonight before the orgy started."

"Wow!" I thought, "Shade! I wish we could stay another week for their staging of Salome." After a trauma like that, it wouldn't surprise me if Tom didn't experience flashbacks while touring the catacombs (the Scavi Tour) under St. Peter's. One never knows when a satyr might leap from the shadows of some sacred spaces and challenge the mood.

It was a trip to puzzle over and enjoy for years. Who were those people in the Keller, anyway? Sadly, the day after, a combo of the winter weather in Vienna and the poor heating in our pension got the better of my immune system and I came down with a head cold. A walk around town brought me to the shingle indicating a doctor's office upstairs. I rode the lift to the second floor, explained my problem, suffered a perfunctory examination, and was finally, led to the doctor's office. There on the desk were hundreds of medicine boxes, some full, some empty, piled high as the Matterhorn. (I didn't know any Austrian mountains to compare it to). The doctor reached gingerly for a box on the bottom, handed it to me, and said in broken English, "Take these and **drink many hot things with much lemons**." As a physician, he was kind of a nebbish. On the other hand, the lemon remark earned him the title of homeopath in my book. For years after, his emblematic advice has made the rounds in my circles of friends. Bless his heart. Now that I think of it, I don't remember seeing a diploma on his wall. Neither 'die Schonen Kunste nor ein Zugelassen Arzt.' Maybe it was under something or other, hard to tell. Nonetheless, I took his advice and I acquired some lemons the next day but without having a hot plate in our hotel room, I let the remedial 'hot things' slide for the time being.

******

Nuns- part 2 (1970)
Love among the ruins
c.f. painting by Argentinian Juan Ibarra "Ruins"

Back story - Once again, the plight of another handicapped gentleman was the agent of change. You recall my work with the mentally handicapped at a summer camp. Well, **Decimo was a slow guy** who worked at NAC as a cameriere. His sister brought him to work and took him home every day. So, when **the faculty decided to let him go** for being intellectually disabled, it sent a shock wave of anger and fear to the other workers. Many of the workers lived with their families on the grounds but they had no contract and no job security. To remedy the immediate situation, my friend Tom circulated a petition to rehire him and the faculty reconsidered their decision and found him another position. Seeing this, the camerieri asked some of us to help them also. With a little back and forth with our college lawyer, an Italian, they obtained the forms for a generic contract which solved the problem without a sciopero (strike) or scandal. As a reward, the workers told the faculty that one of their company vehicles was not worth the maintenance. The college replaced it and I got their old Mercedes to drive. As its new secret owner, I had it painted blue to disguise it, parked it on the grounds, placed a monsignor hat at the back window to avoid tickets, and took my friends, the laundry nuns, on a trip to the mountains, the beach, and restaurants where they cried, never having been in one before in Yugoslavia. Hurray! I remember the first trip we took, seeing them through the rearview mirror, tearing off their veils, breaking out the hair spray, and changing their stockings. School girls on Easter holiday. When vacation came to the college, I happily lent my car to some poor classmates from NAC and the Mexican college. "There I go again, losing vacations through good deeds," I thought. But God wouldn't have it. The **Mother Superior asked me to accompany one of the sisters to Taize - a retreat center**. She placed **two round-trip tickets to Paris** in my hand and a picnic basket.

I was touched by the trust the Mother Superior had in me and I felt protective and solicitous for my "charge" not realizing what a charge she'd turn out to be. But wait, I thought. What would we talk about on such a long journey? "Hello, sister. How's your spiritual life going? Do you have a favorite saint? Does your family keep in touch? Do you like doing laundry?" Having never been on a date I muse to myself just how Jesus might have broken the ice with the Samaritan woman at the well, "Good late afternoon, madam. **Pardon my effrontery but from sources familiar with the case** I'm aware that **you've been married 5 times** and never have been on a date myself, I wonder if you can share with me what was the best pick-up line you've ever heard." "Well, I can tell you, my fine Jewish gentleman, it wasn't, 'Can I borrow your bucket, madam?'" she replied. From my biblical studies, I learned, to my surprise, that wells were typically romantic settings for the Patriarchs and, in this encounter, Jesus was wooing this representative of Sumaria which tolerated the worship of five Baals (lords or husbands) in addition to Yahwah, to win her **back to her covenant with Yahweh, her one true husband**. Knowing this, I realized I wasn't going to get any practical man/woman advice from this story. So, there I was, on my own and tongue-tied.

The week before sister C and I boarded the train, I had lent my car to some Mexican seminarians, leaving me on staycation and free to escort the nun. At the station, the other nuns gave us a bigger basket of food for the journey. We entered the Pullman, stowed the picnic baskets and luggage on the rack, waved to the other nuns and then we took our seats and settled down. At least she settled down. I was so wound up and uber shy that **I jumped at the sound of the train whistle**, as I had done on the dock of the Michaelangelo when its fog horn blasted - "Goodbye, America," three years ago. I confess it's hard to appear macho after screaming, "Oh, God," in full soprano after being startled by sudden noises. I tried my best to recover a smile and confront the situation like a man; well, not exactly like a man but calmly at least. When I regained my composure, I noticed that **she had a nice understanding face**; yes, even a rather pretty one! The longer I looked, the surer I became that the best way to break the ice with sister C. was to share stories about folks who were already in my heart, e.g. mom, my sister, Sister Francine, Conception, Nando Pignatelli, Tom, Ken, Aaron Copland, etc. and she listened. Curiously, on our trip back, she didn't reciprocate by self-disclosing. As a matter of fact, she hardly spoke a word. Curious. Guess my life was nothing to brag about or that she was lost in her thoughts.

Taize was a retreat hub for young people from all over Europe and when we arrived, I helped interpret from French into Italian and Sister C interpreted from German into Italian. I can't begin to tell you how much I admire her. I suggested on our last day that **we use our tickets to Paris and attend mass at Notre Dame.** She agreed. In Paris, we bought souvenirs for her sisters in the convent but I never picked up on how, every time I brought up the subject of other nuns, she'd turn the conversation back to us. Back in Rome, she didn't call me for a week and then one day she told me a Superior from another convent had given her money to treat me to lunch and we went. After lunch, I asked her if she had seen the Borghese Gardens. She hadn't. None of the nuns had the opportunity to sight-see in Rome; they were there to work! While we walked, she asked me if I felt something special in Paris. I said I definitely had a better time than when I took my brothers the year before. They were teens who couldn't speak the language and were bored and frustrated. They wanted to hit on girls and couldn't - what a waste of their time and mine.

Sister C. pressed on, **"But didn't you feel something special?** Like romantic?"

"Well," I said, "It was **Paris** in the spring. True. But romantic? If I did have those feelings, I guess I would have to suppress and get over them ("Very logical, Mr. Spock!")

"You bore, how can you say that? I gave myself to you."

"Well, you must have slipped it under my door," I quipped.

Then the pause, the silence, the painful look, and **it dawned on me, "She's serious**!" What in God's name was I thinking? As the Lord is my witness, I was totally blind-sided by her confession, leagues out of my depth, the tongue-tied, superficial boor that she discovered me to be! Our promenade was over! She turned and walked away and I was too traumatized to run after her and say, "Ah, There's the rub!" I didn't know what to say. I hadn't a clue. In the blink of an eye, I found myself transported into the real world where my sister and brothers had learned how to fend for themselves and remain real under fire. Without combat experience and no ready script to throw out while I gathered my thoughts and responded accordingly, I remained dumbfounded. In hindsight, I realized that what she really needed to hear from me was, "Stay a moment. Stay! Thou art so fair." (words from Goethe's Faust) Even if I didn't mean them, I could even have offered them **on a trial basis to buy me some time to think**. Instead, after shaming her with a flippant remark, I offishly hunkered down in my comfort zone and played the role I knew well – of a cold cerebral Faust to sister C.'s loving Gretchen.

Post Mortem - What was the basic problem here? It was the fact that she was **real** and I hadn't had lessons **on how to be**. It didn't help me after our breakup to hear Nicola di Bari crooning his San Remo hit song on the radio **"La Prima Cosa Bella"** which translates to "I've never seen anything as beautiful in my life as your youthful smile." They played the darn thing over and over again and each time it felt like Thor's Hammer.

After a month, Sister C. and I agreed to meet by the fountain in St. Peter's Square. From there we walked in silence to the huge doors of the Basilica to find a "prete" and a stall where we could confess the sin of flirting. Afterward, we met again at the Bernini fountain (oasis and wells being a favored place where lovers meet in the bible), looked into each other's eyes, and questioned whether what we had done merited confessing. What was there to be sorry for? Maybe if we had sinned on a larger scale as Luther suggested, we would have left with a greater sense of relief, invigorated not by the spray of a fountain plume but by the soothing splash of grace and absolution. Instead, I felt ashamed to have dragged my lady through the empty ordeal of a sacramental gesture. And so, under the righteous noses of the saints atop the colonnades, with a shrug of the shoulders, we smiled and exchanged our first and only kiss, then walked to a bar on the via Conciliazione for a cappuccino, returned to the compound with memories shared and unshared, futures still to be determined, and bachelors again. Sic Transit Gloria Mundi

We learn the Whole of love

The Alphabet–the Words–

A Chapter–then the mighty Book–

Then–Revelation closed–

But in Each Other's eyes–

An Ignorance beheld —---

Diviner then the Childhood's —

And each to each a Child –

Attempted to expound

What Neither — understood–

Alas,that Wisdom is so large–

And Truth–so manifold ! (E.Dickinson)

*****

**So ended my Parson'sTale
My Mission Work on Trial
1967-70
From Jesting to Jousting"**

With one rector down after a student fell climbing into the college,
the new rector (Hickey) was intent on clamping down and regaining

control of his watch. I already had a penchant for turning wine into vinegar when it came to the vice-rector (VR) who only managed to keep his job by the grace of God and the stupidity of the board of directors. Before my first-year summer vacation began, (the vacation I was supposed to forfeit for doing social work with protestants) this second-in-command called a meeting of students interested in doing outreach among the Roman population. Six of us showed up and the VR said he would use his summer to visit seminaries in the U.S. (4 seminaries, I believe) and ask them if they thought a transcultural apostolate (outreach) would be of any benefit to NAC students. What he didn't know was that it was already being done. We would have laughed out loud at him if we didn't fear reprisals and provoke him to shut us down. Well, he came back at summer's end, reconvened the group, and reported that the consensus overseas was that it would be positive, even very positive (sigh of relief) to pursue a transcultural apostolate. But I couldn't leave it alone so I told him, "If you were more involved with what we are doing, this question would never have come up. But since you raised it for argument's sake with others an ocean away as to whether a transcultural apostolate has any value, **my question for you would be, 'Haven't you ever heard of St. Paul?'** Everyone laughed. He turned red. <u>Round One</u>.

The VR didn't follow up for two and a half years but one day, he decided to leave the compound and wander around the city, to pay a visit to the local church (in whose boundaries NAC was located) and see the pastor. There, in the pastor's chair of Santo Spirito in Sassia sat myself, pastor "pro tempore" while the pastor, Don Smerna, was on family business in the south.

"Where is the pastor?"

"You're looking at him."

"You can't be. You're not ordained."

"No. The Jesuits offer Mass. I run the office." Not knowing what to say, he left in a huff. <u>Round Two.</u>

<u>Round three</u> would knock me off my rocking horse. **A month before ordination,** I was summoned to appear before the new rector and VR to be the **first case** of the newly crafted "system of accountability." (Smelled a little like discernment to my educated nostrils). I was accused of unorthodox ideas and unauthorized activities. I figured I would have never passed the dogmatic scrutiny of these conservatives "stick in the muds" but luckily, I had an advocate, a doctoral candidate priest who did a one-on-one interview with me on dogma which I passed. All that was left was my mission work (**gulp**). The VR came at me with guns-a-blazing.

"I have no idea what you do in your free time out there. You never consulted with me," he screamed.

"Father, I remember when you visited Santo Spirito. You saw me covering for its Pastor. You never interviewed me or called me in afterward or telephoned the pastor to comment on my service."

"Wasn't I safe to assume, Father, that you weren't interested or concerned? You said I didn't plug in. **Were you running a parallel pastoral program that I was aware of 'Msgr** and refused to participate in? No? Left on my own then, what was so wrong in finding a local priest and nuns to train me who knew these people better than either of us do?"

"You should have consulted me," he barked.

"Well, think of it this way, to use a Roman example, **if you want to build a colosseum, you need two amphitheaters** to come together. You and I never agreed to do so. Therefore, in the vacuum, I just worked out of my amphitheater."

"Without consulting anyone?" he yelled.

128

"It was during my free time and, by the way, there are at least twenty other students out there doing what I am doing under local supervision and coordination and they're not on the carpet like me. This seems personal, very personal."

"So, you just want to do your own thing. Is that it?"

The bishop raised his hand and stopped the meeting and said, "Well, I see there are some flaws in our system of accountability."

"Bishop," I asked, "What do I tell my family? Should they come to my ordination or not?"

"They can come," he said and we left in silence. You could hear the face of the VR drop to the floor! <u>Knock-out</u>.

P.S. The VR could never have supervised us in the field. His Italian wasn't good enough (for lack of practice).

Six years of minor seminary in Brooklyn, two years of major seminary in Huntington, Long Island and four years of study in Rome - What a long and winding road it proved to be that brought me to my knees in 1971 before the Rector Bishop of NAC to receive the "laying on of hands." On that memorable day, 53 young Americans from all over the United States became priests and were empowered to "say Mass," forgive sins, preach the Gospel, anoint the sick, marry those in love and run Bingo for the lonely and unlucky. As I waited for my turn to be consecrated, I looked around to catch the eye of my five buddies who participated in our unauthorized outreach to the city. Nods and smiles followed. As for the other 48 men, their heads were filled with sugarplum dreams of private Masses with their people while **my group had bigger plans** of **churches filled with family and Italian friends** conducted in two languages with bilingual hymns as well. For us, ordination wasn't a fete for the unfettered (unmarried) in which we agree to be lifelong spiritual bachelor fathers and nothing more. No, indeed, ours was a reunion of field hands celebrating a harvest with a Thanksgiving ritual at which all are seated without rank or distinction in the name of Christ. For our classmates, ordination was a white glove affair. For us, **we were a multi-cultural church family that "was bruised, hurting and dirty for being out in the streets,"** words of Pope Francis. We were children of Vatican II and the pastoral vision of Pope Francis definitely informed our views on ordination. Good shepherds should smell like sheep for being in their midst, says Francis.

So, as I exited St. Peter's after ordination, I was itching to shed the vestments, change to street clothes (we say borghese in Italian) and put on my dancing shoes to party! On the day following my first Mass, my family headed towards Castel Gandolfo (The Pope's timeshare) for a feast of authentic paella prepared and served by the Spanish Nuns of Barcelona, our missionary sisters. Liquor lubricated the tongues of the guests, smiles scaled language barriers, conversations morphed into laughter and "bejesus", that Chiante – it had the bouquet of a fine perfume and we filed out of the banquet well-perfumed and feeling as light as down from the Holy Ghost. A charitable few of our company remained sober enough to serve dinner to the nuns who had hosted us. Then we called it a day. The devil take the dishes!

*****

The Faculty
In Praise of Folly

"Stupidity is a gift from God but it should not be abused." Baron von Bismarck

Let me start with Msgr. Galles, our spiritual director, a rolly-polly Italian-American, a man nothing short of short, an all-around nice guy. We gave him the nickname "Snoopy" after the "Peanuts" character (not the rapper Snoop Dogg). Snoopy roughly translates as "scaccitato" in Italian but, unfortunately, the word has the connotation of someone who snoops around, a sneak, more like a fox than a lovable beagle in the comics. Don't get me wrong, I liked the guy but didn't take him seriously. Not the go-to person in crisis whether personal or spiritual. I couldn't imagine myself knocking on his door and asking "Monsignor Snoopy, I think it's appendicitis. Could you please non-direct me to the nearest hospital?" "Certainly, my son." Before I would even consider consulting a counselor, I'd want to see a sheepskin on his wall. Msgr. Galles was little more than a buddy down the hall.

I caught up with Msgr. Galles one day as we were walking around the inner court of the college, I grabbed a branch from one of the 48 trees honoring each State (Alaska and Hawaii were not represented), and I started whipping myself in jest as we walked. He asked me why and I said that a little flagellation couldn't hurt. He played along.

"What's getting under your skin, my son?" he asked

"Senseless rules, intimidation, power games, and prejudice. Those wounds don't scab over so easily."

He should have replied, "Wow, you sound bitter," but instead, he said, "You should join the student council and change things."

"I'd rather whip myself," I said.

Galles was a more effective counselor with the nuns. Some of the nuns on the compound were practicing extreme forms of mortification such as hair shirts and body hooks and, as their confessor, Snoopy disabused them of such arcane and masochistic practices. What attracted them to him I'm sure was that he was non-threatening and approachable. We, students, however, needed something different in a counselor, someone a little more hard-core and professionally trained. I guess I should mention a pep talk I had with the First Rector. "You're from a big diocese, Brooklyn, and at the top of your class. You're going places," he said. (He thought advancement. I thought placement)

My co-author, Tom, managed to get along much better with the faculty than me. My objectivity and tolerance for the faculty waned and soured after the Vice-Rector, whom I nicknamed Brezhnev, decided to trash the article in, Roman Echoes and so I channeled my energy away from the college.

N.B. In the NAC journal p.44 it said that students "tended to be aloof from community and insisted more on protecting their freedom and developing individual talents. The faculty, on the other hand, was loath to provide actual direction or leadership which would be helpful in the development of individual students." (Aggiornamento p.344) Instead, to reign us in, the new rector instituted procedures aimed at fostering greater student accountability. In other words, trials and I had the honor of being the first test case.

*****

Mission
Mission work is not for the faint of heart
Rome, Italy (1970)

A newly arrived student, who hadn't learned Italian yet, asked me to accompany him to Trastevere to pick out postcards to send home. After we bought them, I took him down to the oratory to meet the kids in the afterschool. When they saw the bag of cards in this American's hand they assumed he brought them treats and rushed him, jumping and grabbing as he held the bag over his head out of reach. We intervened, peeled them away and he ran back to the college. I didn't lay eyes on him again until he fell to his death from atop NAC. To understand the stress he was under, you need to know that **Holy Orders** consists of 7 steps: 4 **minor orders**: reader, porter, acolyte, and exorcist, and 3 **major orders:** sub-deacon, deacon, and priest. We didn't know it at the time but this young man, whom I'll call Mr. Mac, was identified by Prof. Fuchs as having psychiatric problems and Fuchs reported this to the V.R. of NAC, yes, my nemesis we called "Bresnif." The VR then referred this student to Dr. Palermo for treatment. There's where any coordination between the mental health treatment and his advancing to priesthood broke down. While Mr. Mac moved up in minor **orders,** his major psychiatric **disorders** kept pace as ordination loomed larger and ever more ominous. Of course, he never considered telling the faculty. And so, they continued to promote him, pushing him step by step to the breaking point. After his death, **NAC exculpated itself by gas-lighting the suicide as a tragic accident** but we seminarians all knew that no student would have been walking at the site of the fall unless they intended to jump. (Aggiornamento pg.392) Both Tom and I will never forget the night we heard his screams as he fell. Tom ran to Bambino Jesu for an ambulance but there was none available. I managed to get one from Santo Spirito Hospital to pick up the body.

He was a deeply depressed lonely figure ever since he arrived in Rome. Perhaps if he had gotten involved, gotten to know the children of the Oratory (who had startled him that first day), or fellowshipped with us in the mission field, all might have ended differently. He might have enjoyed the kids' company and the stories they shared about themselves and their families between the lessons at afterschool. We did! I remember, for example, how I was blown away by the words of wisdom from a seven-year-old. He seemed quieter and more thoughtful than his compadres. I was preparing him for first communion and we were studying the Ten Commandments when I introduced the commandment about stealing. We talked about it, gave examples and then I asked him whether gambling was a form of stealing and therefore wrong. To my surprise, he said no, it was manly and gutsy "as long as you didn't go overboard, for instance, eating is good if you don't overdo."

So, I pressed him, "Why is gambling good?"

He said, "Because when you gamble you care enough about the truth to put money on it. You take a stand."

Wow! I think that the lad earned himself a seat at the card table of independent thinkers where the basic requirements are some chips (ideas) a chair, and a gambler's heart, I think St. James said something along these lines (about backing up one's faith with action) as did Kierkegaard.

Making my rounds

Being in Rome, housed in a gated community, living among your countrymen, with food, lodging, and transportation all provided, this should have been sufficient compensation for the faculty staffing a sinecure like N.A.C. But, when one throws in an open bar and a cache of liquor – I'm talking Johnny Walker Black Label and Punt e Mes, and Courvoisier etc. I think this calls for a luxury tax on their own liquor. If the faculty caught us, stealing their stash and ask us why, we would have replied, "The Master has need of it." And so, **around the holidays when the poor could use some love** and lift, my crew and I made a few impromptu dumbwaiter trips to the faculty's cellar, filled several suitcases with selected spirits, and filed out of the compound with a **libation and declaration** for the families we served that year, "The American Church loves you." I had just returned to Rome after attending the funeral of my grandfather state-side, but, before I left for Europe, I dispatched tourist postcards from the JFK airport to families on my list.

After a few days of rest and grieving, I set out with my suitcase of contraband on my pastoral visits. I knocked on a door in the Borgo Pio Quarter with a bottle pulled from the suitcase and was careful to prevent the other booze in my bag from rattling and declared, "The American Church loves you."

"Thank you, father," she said. "Please come in. He's gone."

"Who's gone?" I asked.

She took the bottle and called, "Senora, the Padre e qui."

Another woman appeared and said, "He's gone. He's gone. Come this way."

"Who's gone?"

The next thing I knew, I was standing in an adjacent room, and there on the mattress with a candle burning at each corner of the bed was Lorenzo in a suit. Guess what the family presumed? That I came on the heels of my thoughtful postcard. I had just gotten off the plane, stopped at the duty-free store to buy them brandy, and then made it straight to their house in time to bless the dead. All I knew was that Lorenzo was gone, a miracle was being claimed which kept God in the picture and now I needed a drink more than either Lorenzo or his family did, bless their hearts! Nonetheless, I resisted opening the suitcase for fear that if I did, we'd all be laid out and as unresponsive as Lorenzo! Gadamer says that we are never impartial observers. The way we approach situations includes our history, our values, our reason for being there, and the interpretive lens we chose. In other words, we always bring baggage with us though we try to prevent it from rattling to keep our secrets under wraps.

The passing of Lorenzo Lanza was a sad and unforeseen inflection in an otherwise joyful season that runs **from the visit of Babbo Natale to**

the departure of la Befana, the gift-bearing witch. It was a grim and painful reminder that life includes both feast and famine, a mix of wine and vinegar that even Lord Jesus found repugnant in his final hours. Strange to say, despite the tragedy, despite the shock and grief involved, the Lanza family found angels in the details, namely the providential visit of a churchman such as I, a Johnny on the spot, who wasn't walled up in a rectory or college or lost in otherworldliness, but here to lend his sympathy and give his time as Christ did to Martha and Mary when Lazaras died. Ask this family about my impromptu appearance and they would have called it **a miracle**, no bones about it. (I shouldn't say bones given the circumstances).

Frankly, I saw my "chance visit" as being more coincidental than providential, given its backstory. For one thing, I had only recently met this family and added them to my Xmas list as an afterthought. Consequently, I actually felt embarrassed to be with them now at such a pivotal moment in their lives. Secondly, I wished to God that I had sent them a postcard of New York's St. Patrick's Cathedral in keeping with the season **instead of one of the Empire State** Building which was frankly a gaudy 3-D piece of tourist fodder. Last and worst of all, my Xmas gift, a bottle of brandy, which would have been fine at an Irish wake but as stolen property, that basket of cheer was hardly a gift of the Magi! Larceny aside, and known only to me, I was certainly received as an honored and respected guest on par with the jolly Christmas elf and a strega with a broom. "Bite your tongue and play the part," I told myself. "It's the right thing to do!" I knew what Don Camilo, the make-believe priest in pulp fiction, would do in my place. He'd probably blurt out, "Porca la Miseria" on seeing the body, then gather what wits he had, and pray the rosary with them. So that was what I did, exactly as St. Paul advised, and wept with those who wept and ministered in season and out of season (in this case Christmas season). I stayed an hour and prayed with the family, then said my goodbyes and mindlessly wished them a

Merry Xmas (damn customs and Tiny Tim). Looking back, I guess the episode was a classic example torn from the pages of sacramental theology, a **case of "ex opere operato" where the good deed is nobler than the minister** who performs it. If that's true, my visit probably was a miracle because "where two or more are gathered together in His name," etc. You know what that means - all the boxes have been checked and despite my callousness, it was a loving thing to do. It didn't make me St. Francis, but a humbler servant for sure and if it wasn't a miracle, it was at least an **eucatastrophe**.

"Coincidences are **spiritual puns**"- wrote G. K. Chesterton.

****

More Than I Could Stomach
And Less Than Meets The Eye

I came in late to the college for lunch one day after ministering to a patient in Santo Spirito Hospital and my tardiness earned me the dubious "honor" of sitting at the faculty table for lunch. Having nothing of substance to say, I proposed that during our upcoming summer stay at Castel Gandolfo, the brass would host picnics and team-building games involving faculty and student body for fun and fellowship. I nearly choked at my suggestion but I was saved by some unexpected and frankly welcome objections from our fearless leaders.

"The menu would be a problem for me," said the Dean. "I'm a vegetarian and it might dampen the festivities if I had to keep asking my table mates to pass me the carciofi, the gnocchi, the grapes, etc., every two minutes."

The others laughed. "Well, there better not be seafood on the menu or someone will be driving me to the infirmary," added another genius. Then came the piece de resistance from the Rector. He had an annoying nasal voice that whined like a dentist's drill. As a matter of fact, his father was a dentist

"I hear what you're saying gentlemen," the rector told the group, "Diets can be tricky things." (And old coots can be picky things, I thought.) He continued, "My family knew for years that my mother was allergic to eggs. However, we were never really sure if her aversion was psychological or physiological." (This was decades before **PTED post-traumatic egg disorder** was recognized by the DSM) "So," he continued, "We added some egg white to her broth and she had a terrible reaction." Everyone nodded. Except for me who thought, "Wow! A picnic with these guys would unmistakably feature one of the longest **Whine** lists in dining history!"

So, I said, "Ya know, your Excellency, the last time I tried to poison my mother, she harped on it for weeks." Silence! I excused myself and left to grab a snack. When I finally had a car of my own, I learned that our nuns on campus had no digestive issues and were chafing in their habits for picnics and getaways to the seashore, the mountains, and places of historical interest, etc. We had some wonderful times together.

Our Mission Team in Rome

Our Mission Team Parish Team (1970)

A wise man (aka Jesus) once warned us not to entrust newly pressed wine to aging bota bags lest the leather would rupture and the wine would be lost. Despite their love and good intentions toward the youth of Santo Spirito parish, Don Smerna and the Spanish nuns ignored this advice by insisting on using wineskins past their expiration date with the children. It fell to us seminarians to house the church's legacy in new barrels capable of containing the juices and hormones of the next generation who would make up the body of Christ.

Example 1) One Christmas season a kid from our group who prided himself on being a communist and wore a red handkerchief around his neck thought it funny to position the statues of Mary and Joseph in a compromising proximity and posture within the manger scene. **"Which one of you committed sacrilege**?" shouted Don Smirna. The guilty party wasn't even capable of lying let alone blasphemy so he confessed. It took some tact and an apology to restore peace on earth that Xmas. The poor kid cried and turned as red as his neck kerchief - Sic transit gloria mundi, kid. Bless your heart, comrade

Example 2) It was a Good Friday like no other Don Smirna was manning the pulpit and Tom and I were honor guards standing on opposite sides of the church next to the front pews and supposedly setting the tone on this solemn occasion. We did well up until the sermon but we weren't prepared for what was to come. **"I've been to the Holy Land," Don Smirna began,** "and I can vouch that they are everywhere, at every corner, at every turn. You can't avoid them contaminating the marketplace, molesting infants and children, preying on men sweating and toiling in the heat of mid-day, and torturing shoppers and visitors alike with their incessant droning. You know what I'm talking about.

They're everywhere, FLIES, my friends. Yes, flies. Clouds of them buzzing around the head of our blessed Lord, his hand nailed to the cross beams impotent to brush them away from his painful crown or pluck them from his blood-sealed eyes." Wow, we never expected that. It took all our self-control not to burst into peals of laughter and scandalize the pious soul squirming in their pew glued to every poetic and graphic detail of the talk. We ran down the aisle, hands over our mouths until we made it out the door and exploded. This was not Baroque. This was Rocco Cuckoo. An old woman coming in late asked us what was happening. We said, "Just another gothic gem of a sermon by Padre Smirna, that's all." Thank God, the kids didn't witness our impiety! We walked away thinking, "Smirna just **turned Good Friday into Good Flyday**, for Pete's sake!" Or maybe he just got Jesus mixed up with **Orestes**?

Example 3) Vestiges of this particular debuncle found their way to the Spanish nuns' parochial agenda without discussion – in the form of a bus trip for the kids of the parish to the Shrine of St. Rita (DOB 1381). Curious fact about this saint, she was exhumed 3 times, and every time her body was as intact and uncorrupted as on the day of her burial. Furthermore, during her lifetime she received a partial stigmata conferred while she was embracing a crucifix. One of its thorns became dislodged and planted itself on her forehead. During her three disinterments, fresh blood miraculously exuded from that wound. Her life was not a happy one, to say the least. She was forced to marry, suffered years of domestic abuse, and had two children in a perilous time. Still, over the years, her husband mellowed and became a good man under her influence only to be murdered in an intra-family feud. The whole town was shocked when she pardoned his murderers, something which her sons refused to do. **She was actually relieved when the black plague struck down her sons** before they could exact revenge or justice, you decide and earn themselves a seat in hell. Need I go on?

This is an incredible story, strong on doctrine and less strong on parenting skills or as an appropriate role model for battered women (the devil is indeed in the details). I wonder whether sharing those details wouldn't have sparked some bare-knuckle discussion between the kids and nuns if they picked over this history of St Rita with a fine tooth comb? On our way back home, the bus stopped for a picnic, the highlight of the trip. The area we picked, however, was full of briars, and every time a kid was pricked, he or she knew enough of the legend to target their curses. "D_m you, St. Rita,**Dannazione a las espinas**." It was, I suppose, a sad day for religious education and an uninspiring pilgrimage, or maybe not.

Part of our role as co-workers with Pastor Smerna and the nuns was to promote peace and cooperation among the adult players, to offer alternatives to failed interventions, to love and connect with the children through services delivered with a gentle touch, to foster sportsmanship at play and ethics for the day to day, etc. Although there was nothing special to see at the shrine of St. Rita, just a lot of old ladies lighting candles, we were afforded plenty of teaching moments on the bus.

One of the kids, the self-styled communist, whined, "What's the use of saying the rosary? I don't get anything out of it."

I asked him, "Do you think God is smart?"

"Yeah."

"So, why would you insult him by reciting words that make no sense to you?

Have a real conversation, and ask Him to make you a better and happier you. (Mario Puzo's book 'The Godfather' had just been published and so, I plagiarized it in the service of prayer).

"If you are at a loss for what to say, son," I told him. "Close your eyes and imagine this scene. Pretend you are a soldier in the Mafia meeting with the Godfather. You kneel and ask for his guidance and say, "I'm sorry for screwing up in the past and swear never to betray the familia again. Amen."

My little friend just smiled at my gangster version of the Our Father." So I asked him the big question, "Do you think God cares?"

"Yes."

"How do you know?"

"He died for us."

"Right, and He works miracles for those who ask for spiritual guidance in good faith. Don't treat Him like a genie, a cash cow. He knows what you really need to be perfect and it often involves sacrifice. Ask in good faith and He will grant it. Good question, comrade!"

I had to chuckle when I remembered how he admonished Sister Maria Jesus earlier saying, "Stop trying to drag me into heaven. I'm not ready yet!" (a fun-size version of St. Augustine's complaint, "Save me Lord but not just yet.") After we started the oratory, we realized that these kids needed more than math and reading skills and so besides after-school tutoring and, in addition to parish outings, we added Bible study and youth Masses celebrated by Fr. Arias, Masses which were age-appropriate, tailored for growth and fun.

As missioners, **we worked as a team** when possible. I remember visiting an elderly couple who had been faithfully living together "in sin" for 50 years. We bonded. The guy was a former nightclub performer. He taught me to play a piece on guitar and so I returned to the States as a one-tune minstrel. The following year, however, another seminarian, a friend of Tom, picked up where I left off and, in the end, he arranged for and attended their wedding. Nice Surprise! No wedding cake for you, Satan!

Example 4) This one has to do with an attack on the Oratorio by local thugs and Don Smirna's solution. Cherry bombs were sent over the gates of the oratory and the nuns hurried the frightened children out a back way while Tom secured the place from potential vandals. Eventually, those hoodlums doubled around, found Tom trying to escape, blackened his eye, and chased him to the church. Tom pounded on the door. Smyrna let him in, secured the door, ran to the back room, and came back **with a gun**! Tom refused the Neapolitan solution and phoned the police who came and defused the situation. Tom lost his chance for martyrdom. SCHADE! But he's still young.

Example 5) The Italian Audiences - Breaking News – Italians can be a tough crowd to please! If you don't believe me just ask any impresario back in the heyday of the Coliseum how the crowd reacted when their MC announced, "We're out of lions!" Even Don Rickes couldn't finesse such a mob.

******

Make 'm Laugh

Truth be told, **at times** we were no more adept at managing or second-guessing the kids from the Oratory than the nuns were. On my third summer in Rome, my team organized **an activity day** for them at NAC's vacation residence **at Castel Gandolfo**. It was to be a day of games, sports, food, and entertainment. Nando Pignatelli, a former circus clown and acrobat, was asked to perform dressed as a native American in chaps, and war paint, sitting by his teepee facing a crackling campfire. That was what we planned. We thought it was cool. The kids thought it was infantile and acted out by hurling insults calling him out as a phony Indian and trying to make him step out of his role and speak Italian. Finally, to our surprise and horror, the kettle of back and forth reached a boiling point and they grabbed him hand and foot and carried him towards the fire shouting, "We'll make you talk!" We immediately stepped in, scolding them, "What are you doing? Are you crazy?"

In the end, they apologized, we smoothed Nando's "ruffled feathers," passed the peace pipe, and Nando gave one hell of a good show. **Nando,** who was born **on New Year's Day,** celebrated that event every year by **jumping off a bridge** into the Tiber when he came of age, whereupon a buddy would fish him out and bring him to shore.

"Why do you do this?" I asked him.

"Porque e bello," he would answer (Because it is beautiful). His choice of words struck me as strange and somewhat feminine but **beautiful** is a strong and non-uni gender expression in Italian. In fact, my manly uncle, Willie used the word BEAUTIFUL to describe how he felt when asked "Come stai?" How are you, Willie?

If the episode of Nando and the Kids struck **you** as "barbaric," chances are you've never attended the opera in Italy or watched a Fellini movie. I remember being in a small town but big enough to have a theater where I could see a performance of **Verdi's Macbeth.** I remember watching the maintenance crew rushing to clear the vegetables off the stage after Act I. The opera proceeded with the occasional catcalls and whistling but reached a breaking point in Act IV when a coven of pasta-enriched dancers cavorted clumsily around the swooning body of Macbeth. (I hoped the choreographer had already left town for his good). Finally, thank God, the dancers exited stage right when the lead crone tripped behind the curtain causing a pileup of thuds and curses which brought the audience to its feet applauding and shouting, "Bis. Bis. Do it again," and the troupe repeated their routine da capo. Pardon the puns but this was the most **spellbinding**, enchanted, spontaneous, and **cathartic** performance of Verdi's Macbeth I had ever seen. Not only did the audience get their money's worth but they left the theater pondering which vegetables to buy for the next show.

Let me just share what we took away from our misreading the kids' psyches at the Castel Gandolfo. We decided to go with their strengths. Gilbert and Sullivan once wrote, "Let the punishment fit the crime." We decided to use a more affirmative approach and "Let the devil have his due." **I invited** a group of **kids to dinner** in Trastevere **at** a restaurant called **Da Cencio**, La Parolaccia where the waiters were dressed in prisoners' stripes and badgered, heckled, and otherwise insulted the guests. They would crawl under your table saying, "Here kitty, kitty, kitty. Come here you d–m cat!" Whenever a lady from the local escort service walked through the door with her date, they'd serenade the unlucky couple with "Here comes the bride," and gift them a bottle of Asti Spumante plus lessons on how to uncork the bottle cork manually. They would throw your silver on the table and complain and act annoyed at every request you made. Can you imagine how much the kids relished acting out in such a setting? The only socially redeeming aspect of the evening was in teaching the kids who didn't already know, how to twirl their spaghetti using a spoon and a fork. Nobody ordered osso buco! These kids out-grossed the waiters and half the guests. **I was so proud**! We left the place laughing, stuffed, validated, and bonded. We gave these devils their due. Veni. Vidi.Vici **– We came, we saw, we conquered!**

Years later, when I was a missionary in Argentina, I learned the wisdom of providing spaces and occasions to **"let slip the dogs" of our dark side**. Moreno, the inventor of Psychodrama, had a theater of spontaneity in Vienna and the woman who played leading roles there caught the eye and heart of a man in the audience who, after attending several shows, asked for her hand in marriage. Months later, he returned to Moreno's theater and swore and shouted at him for deceiving him.

"She's nothing like the girl I saw on stage," he yelled. "She curses like a sailor, has a foul disposition, and is physically abusive. What do you think of that?"

"I think you should bring her back here and let me work with her," said Moreno. For months, he had her play the part of criminals, hussies, and prostitutes with the result that in time, she was able to be a hellian on stage and a loving wife at home. I wasn't surprised. That's why they allow Fasching and Karneval in Germany and Mardi Gras here – to unleash the snarling dog inside us **once a year**.

Part III

Back in the USA

Back in the USA (1971)
Reunions

After I returned from Italy, I made sure to reconnect with and thank Canon Bill Johnson, my professor of Anglican Theology in Rome. He convinced me to join him as a professor at his Institute of Theology at The Cathedral of St. John the Divine NYC. Spoiler: After four years of working together he convinced me to answer a call for an Anglican missionary in Argentina and to be received into the Episcopal Church as a priest and I did.

Once back home from Rome, I also made it a point to visit Sister Francine, the Clinical Social Worker who supervised me as a teenager. Finally, I also re-connected with my friend Tom Kirshberg who was serving in the Peace Corps in Ethiopia. I telegraphed him out of concern for his safety and we renewed and deepened our friendship. I have attached the telegram I sent him.

In the States, I settled into my 1st parish. I still hadn't unpacked my feelings about that separation from sister C and I was totally unprepared for the overwhelming pain that would overtake me that year. It finally dawned on me that like Sister "C," I had also given myself to her but didn't know it. Romeo said, "Stone walls cannot keep love out." He obviously never visited the Vatican or maybe he did. Yes, for much of my first year at home, I had to force a smile when I remembered her as Guilietta Massina did in the final scene of "Cabiria." I hoped that like Cabiria some reveler would tease away my tears and get me back on track. How desperately I prayed that Our Lord would pull me from the hole I had fallen in and give me a heart of service. In many ways and after several years, He did.

Nuns Again?

My next strange encounter with nuns is not worth mentioning, so I will. As a junior priest in my 1st parish, I expected to say mass, counsel in Spanish, preach in Portuguese and Italian, and run BINGO in my spare time. Given that over 60% of the parishioners at Pius V spoke Portuguese, I enrolled in courses at Berlitz and meanwhile, got by with Spanish. Then, as luck would have it, I discovered that living at our convent was a young Portuguese nun who taught French at a local high school and who might be willing to correct my sermons and rein in my Italian accent. We connected immediately and exchanged stories of Europe, of languages, and, of course, acculturation. I gave her my article to read and she was very impressed. One Saturday afternoon, I brought my sermon for her to scan and found all the other nuns toasting her. It was her birthday.

"Make a toast, Father," they chimed.

"Okay, here's to two of the nicest words I know in Portuguese – Ines Axxxxx (I said her name)." Applause, guffawing, and done. When I came back for the sermon that evening, she was home alone.

"Where are the others?"

"Out."

"Out, on your birthday? Did you speak to your parents in Canada?"

"Yes. It was nice."

"Did you have a cake?"

"No, just champagne."

"Well, we can fix that! I'll be back." On my return, I handed her a box of cupcakes and birthday candles to share with the other nuns.

"That is very nice," she chanted and leaned forward to give me a kiss. I offered my cheek but she had other plans and gave me an unsolicited French lesson bouche à bouche that Berlitz couldn't match. I didn't enjoy it. I couldn't, because I was sucking on a Halls lozenge. I was literally cocked for sororicide and ready to fire (True Story). Had I coughed, I trust that the Diocesan Tablet would have delivered a sanitized version of the incident "Nun's in Pius V convent passed away peacefully despite valiant efforts of assistant pastor to revive her by mouth to mouth resuscitation." When the ambulance arrived the priest was observed fighting back the tears while administering Extreme Unction. "The Enquirer" would have a different take altogether, "Nun dies of Halls-a tosis in the arms of a priest," cause of death – PTSD, Post Tablet Swallowing Disorder." Needless to say, (so, I'll say it) such reporting couldn't fail but to trigger in me a different brand of PTSD (Post Tabloid Swallowing Disorder), a condition that plagues me to this day.

From that scare and potential disaster going forward, I decided to edit my own sermon and have my blood serum checked for iron to explain my magnetism with nuns. I still get chills every time the TV blares, "RICOLA," making me recall a certain Ines Axxx, a polyglot, a fun-size interpreter, and a way beyond-the-pale FRENCH teacher with a weakness for authors with a full head of hair like me back then. And Albert Camus.

Sister Francine

I never share my Lozenger story with Ines and spoil the romantic moment as I did with sister 'C.'

As I said, once back in Brooklyn, I rushed to pay a visit to Sister Francine of the Nursing Sisters of the Sick Poor to thank her for having introduced me to the mission and social work as a teen volunteer in a summer camp for people with Down's Syndrome. After four years apart, we had some serious catching up to do. We talked for an hour swapping stories, then she asked if I could spend a few minutes speaking with another nun who was getting her master's in history but who had never been out of the country. (I will dub her "Nun the Less" after St. James – the Lesser and dub my friend Francine, "Nun – the Greater," for obvious reasons.)

"Well," said I, "After living in Rome, I feel duty bound to consider any friend of the goddess Clio as a friend of mine. Make the introductions." (Orson Welles couldn't have phrased it better)

Francine hollered upstairs and I heard the clatter of nun shoes on the wood floor above and a moment later, I heard a throaty, "Hello, Father! How does it feel to be back in the States?"

I replied, **"I feel like a fish out of mineral water!"**

She laughed. "Bet you'll be missing 'La Dolce Vita' over there - the wine, women, and songs," she continued.

"Frankly, sister, I don't remember singing that much in Rome," I replied. Francine rolled her eyes.

"OK, Don Giovanni," she cautioned, "No tall tales right now. Sister M wants to tap your brain for information and advice." I have to admit that Francine's reproach was unexpected and it stung a little in front of a stranger. I wasn't sure whether she was reining me in, ringing me out, insulting me or just being playful. But one thing was for sure, I was outnumbered. Nun-the-Less sat down beside me, shook my hand, gave me the once over, and began,

"I'd like to hear your stories. I'm sure they're interesting, but first I'm curious to know how you managed to stay thin after four years of eating pasta?"

Wow, didn't see that coming. I was just about to counterattack with, "Isn't it a little late in the hunger game to be asking me such a question, my round little friend?" (Sorry, there goes that misogyny again!)

On the other hand, my old school nuns would have labeled her a **Bold Piece** for asking such a question. Pretty bold for a first meeting? You'd think she knew me for years! Wait a minute! Just a darn minute (I did a double take and looked closer at her) and wondered to myself, "Am I being hoodwinked? Is this my sister Margie again in disguise? Am I being T-boned by the unexpected like mom was? Nah, it couldn't be. Relax. Shake it off. Take the high road, holster your gun, and just answer the question.

*****

The science of eating
(Mangia)

"To be honest, I have to give the Italians credit for knowing how to orchestrate healthy meals. Even the big Sunday lunch begins early and unrushed, starting with an aperitif (digestivo) to get the juice flowing, then some light broth with strands of angel hair added, a salad with enough olive oil to coat the stomach and rein in the effects of the wine, then the **primo,** or first course usually, pasta **followed by** the **secondo or** the main course of meat or fish after which the diner could choose a piece of fruit or a wedge of gorgonzola, and wind down with a dessert liquor, or gelato, or pastry then pulling into the roundhouse, and cap the afternoon with, a rich demitasse of espresso or cappuccino. It's a three-hour journey during which there isn't a trace of that American "all you can eat" attitude.

Throughout the afternoon, the Italian food train makes many stops, allowing for conversation and a chance to stretch your legs. When we're finished, we clear the table, break out the cards, or watch soccer and catch our breath. The food is fresh and unprocessed. (Unlike what I ate at my mom's during my first week back home when I pigged out on Entenmann's cake and burgers and gained 10 lbs.)"

"Bottom line, Sister, if you want to get svelte, move to Italy for several months, take some cooking classes, then come back, and locate your neighborhood fresh markets and reap the benefits." (Thus, spake me the connoisseur.)

Nun-the-less remarked, "Well, you've clearly left your heart in those Roman trattorias!" Maybe in Angie's homey one where, if you came in before diner time, you might see freshly made fettuccine draped like a shawl over the back of a chair drying for the day.

(As to my heart, I left it in the NAC convent along with my umbrella and two canceled tickets to Paris, but let's continue.)

Alora!

With small talk over, she got down to business. "Do you think that a person who never gets to travel abroad can still become a good history teacher?" (Evidently, her vow of poverty was coming back to bite her in her career.)

"Of course," I chirped. "You don't have to be an astronaut to do astronomy. Galileo wasn't one but it didn't stop him from discovering the ring around Saturn. And, as you know, Emily Dickinson met more worlds working out of her backyard than most travelers do in a lifetime." (To tell the truth, I was nervous counseling her.) Had it been 10 years later, I would have suggested watching Sr. Wendy, the British art critic and a nun who shocked TV audiences on both sides of the pond with her worldly and risqué comments on fine art. She was comfortable in her sexuality but admitted temperamentally she would have made a terrible wife. She would have been a perfect role model of a self-confident professional woman, worth more than a thousand of my puny words of encouragement. Sr. Wendy might have bolstered Nun-the-Less's self-esteem into taking a quantum leap from the posture of a timid anchorite to an assertive and expressive anchor-woman like Rachael Maddow, all in a single bound. I don't know what the fates eventually had in store for Nun-the-Less, they say that all roads eventually lead to Rome. I hope hers did! I hope she may have had the opportunity to visit the Eternal City at least once and stay long enough for the magic of Roma to charm her. But, if you are still then fighting the battle of the bulge, my dear Nun-the-Less, take my advice, moderate the pasta, say "no" to gnocchi, steer clear of lasagna, (if you want less-on-ya (pun) bones, put less-on- your plate) or else you may find yourself salivating every time you hear the word **"Ciao" in Rome** and register it as a summon to the nearest 'Chuck Wagon.'

*****

Seize life but chew food slowly
Devour the elephant a bite at a time!
(Carpe Diem sed Festina Lente-)

At home, I'd wolf a pizza slice in less than 60 seconds,

But in Rome, I'd embrace each margarita when languidly she beckons.

At home, I'd sip the altar wine, then mourn my sins and purge them.

Now, I bring flasks to Tuscany and shamelessly submerge them.

Before, I'd pass a flower stands and never smelled the roses.

But here, I'd charge a friend's corsage, despite what shock that causes.

(ME)

Pros and cons of spending years in a foreign-speaking country

"Travel is good but not essential," I continued. "It enabled a sheltered guy like me to become a public figure, a clergyman. It helped Johannes Brahmns to incorporate Hungarian Dances into his repertoire and to champion and help publish the non-Germanic music of Czech composer Antonin Dvorak. But for someone like **Paul Gauguin**, travel only offered him an opportunity to exploit the ignorance of his Western audiences by promoting French Polynesia as a demi-paradise which it wasn't. **His exotic paintings** that garnered him fame **were not of Polynesia** at all **but of Samoa** copied from photographs. These were presumed to be authentic from 1899 until recently, when an indigenous modern artist, Yuki Kihara, recognized the faces and the plants in these paintings as Samoan, and he slammed Gaugin for another scam, i.e. for neglecting to mention to tourists the violence, colonial scars, the climatic disasters that assailed the Polynesians which **he did know** first-hand." (from an article published in CNN 4/22/2022)

In short, I confessed to sister Nun-the-Less, our historian-in-training, that for me, living in Rome was indeed transformative, not for the things I learned. (historical knowledge, the customs, and the culture of Italy). Such goodies were tangential at best! No sorellina, it was for the things I unlearned and a place to *come of age*. It was an opportunity for me to be open, vulnerable, and grow under the catalyst of unfamiliar surroundings into becoming a child again, learning to speak and walk unaided. It enabled me to reclaim parts of the heritage that I never knew or dismissed out of hand and thereby allowed me to take off national blinders, shake my bridle loose, and traces as I watched cultural worlds collide like tectonic plates (Gadamer) causing both quakes and some shuffling of the cards. Best of all, I experienced this as a carefree scholarship student in my 20s. How lucky can one get? It's certainly better to come of age before age comes upon you.

*****

My First Parish
Homecoming Assignment 1971

When I came back to the USA as a new priest, I paid an obligatory visit (after family and friends) to my home parish of St. Jerome to say mass with **Bishop Mulroney** the pastor and former English professor at my undergraduate Alma Mater, the Seminary of the Immaculate Conception, Huntington Long Island N.Y. He told me that to get off on the right foot in the priesthood I should apprentice to an older priest, a father figure as he did when he was newly ordained. I said, "No thanks. I have had four years of excellent supervision from Roman clergy in the field and I think I'm ready as I'll ever be."

At that point, he heard some disturbance in the parlor and asked what that could be. I said that I brought Alida back with me from Rome.

"Let's open it up," he suggested.

"BISHOP, you misunderstood. I said Alida – **Alida Pignatelli** and her Mom, Mima **not** a liter of **wine**. They're staying with me at my mom's house." He was not pleased. This was my last encounter with this surrogate father figure and I, the prodigal who shunned his embrace.

When I went to get **my assignment** from the Ordinary Bishop of the Diocese, I found him holding in his hand a letter from Rome sent by the pastoral counselor at NAC which read, "We're sending you six fine new priests and one troubled one."

"That must be me," I said.

"Only one parish is willing to take a chance on you," said the bishop.

"How many parishes will the other guys get?" I asked

"One each," he replied.

"Then, we're good," I said. "I accept the assignment and **I promise to do my best as always.**" The bishop's tepid reception of my positive attitude was a bit disconcerting but I was becoming used to being underrated by the hierarchy.

I was sent to the parish of Pius V in Jamaica Queens N.Y. The pastor of the place was a tall athletic Irishman (circa 65 years old) and no stranger to drink, who prided himself on being an African American advocate (he called himself the "black priest" despite having no accomplishments to justify that claim.) I am sure that his heart was in the right place when he invited the Black Panthers to run groups in the parish, but that stunt didn't sit well with his conservative Black parishioners at Pius V, who forthwith banished them and their "racist' propaganda campaign from holy Catholic ground. The same way that our patron St. Pius V broke the grip of the Ottoman Empire on Europe and routed the Turks.

Fr. Joe introduced **my first Christmas sermon** by saying with slurred speech and unmodulated volume **"Don't give them BS,** young man." Tom the curate and the congregation cringed. I preached a homily in which the three wise men, one old, one middle-aged, and one young visit the infant Jesus one at a time. They each saw the new king as being their exact age and came away gratified. But after their comparing notes, they realized their stories didn't jive, so they re-entered the stable together and saw Jesus as he was-a baby, accessible to all.

Moral: As St. Irenaeus, the Doctor of Unity (Pope Francis just gave Irenaeus this title) admonishes us "Don't make Jesus in your image. It is when we come together that we see him as he is 'God's eternal Youth and Lordship.'" Pastor Joe was so pleased with my sermon and so drunk that he jumped over the altar rail as if it were a tennis net to shake my hand.

I also remember when he found the relic of Pius V in a huge Brass reliquary and brought it to the hospital to bless Ms. Pearl, a parishioner's mother. He was so drunk that he misjudged the distance and **clobbered her** on the head, knocking her down in bed. Then forgetting what he did, he bopped her a second time bumped into an orderly, gave him the bent arm salute, and left on the cloud he came on. I thought, "Thank God for celibacy. May this Mule of a man remain in reproductive Limbo all his remaining days." (or words to that effect).

One final vignette – Our housekeeper Ms. Sweney, an intellectually challenged Irish spinster who used to listen in on my phone calls surreptitiously, had to go to the funeral of a relative in L.A. **Knowing how rowdy Irish funerals can be, Fr. Joe wished her "Have a good time, Mary."** She scowled and mumbled something on the way out. When she returned the following week and opened the rectory's back door, Pastor Joe was lying in state. He had died the previous morning while preparing for mass having unwisely decided to go bowling with his buddies the night before while still on the mend from the flu. Big mistake, Big Guy! Joe was not a bad sort really but like Piglet, he had a very little brain.

The other chap in the rectory was a forty-year-old curate, Tom, who was in charge of the youth. He was a conservative and a body-builder who connected and engaged with young people with a love of both the Bible and his barbells. He spent most of his days off walking along the beach, at the gym, or shooting hoops. How did the three of us get along? (Make that two after Joe's demise) famously and responsibly as a team.

But when the free time cue ball was launched, we scattered across the felt in search of a pocket to drop into usually the family home. This was typical in many rectories I am told. Frankly, **we never signed up to be Monks!**

Insight into our detachment: In the States, I once led a group exercise that included laity and clergy in which the participants were asked to pick four out of a list of five passengers they would choose to share space in their lifeboat after their luxury liner sank. These were the categories, a doctor, a handyman, a navigator, a policeman, or a priest. It was a large group and one couldn't find a significant and recognizable pattern of preferences among the participants except in the case of priests. The priests **never** chose to have a fellow priest in the lifeboat with them. Feel free to hypothesize! Finally, I give the Diocese credit for assigning me to a parish of outlanders where I'd come off as one of the boys.

Update: After Three Years of "trying my best" at St. Pius V, I threw in the purificator and took a five-year sabbatical, before accepting an offer from my friend Canon Bill Johnson —to be an Episcopalian Missionary in Argentina

*****

Part IV

Argentina

New mission Buenos Aires
New continent, New Language, New World
(Argentina 1980-1983)

As an Episcopal priest Confronting my Bishop

Sad to say, guys wearing purple shirts were no better in Argentina (1980-1983). I was by then an Anglican priest, more mature and with theology degrees and four years of teaching under my belt. I fully expected to do better as a seasoned minister in South America than I had as a student in Rome. When I arrived in **Buenos Aires, the country was still under the control of the military Junta**. Protests against the regime generally resulted in arrests or being abducted and **thrown to one's death from a plane**. The only protests tolerated by the government were weekly gatherings of a few hundred grandmothers marching around the Plaza de Mayo every Wednesday with placards showing photos of the "disappeared." The only thing we as missionaries could do to protect people was to visit prisons and make a list of those detained in the hope that our record keeping would forestall a fatal plane ride. I partnered with a fellow missionary from England. One day, I learned that he had disappeared. I asked our bishop what happened. He told me that he had sent the guy packing back to England when he learned that this missionary had joined Amnesty International. His Excellency justified his decision by saying, **"We shouldn't be involved in politics."** Oh my God, **where did I hear that rubbish before?** To be blunt, this bishop was not the brightest. I heard that It took him an extra two years to get through seminary. He only got to be a priest and later a bishop **based on his father's reputation** as a prominent Swiss-Argentine businessman, a member of the English-privileged class of Argentines, and quite prosperous before Peron nationalized British businesses. But this son of his has none of his father's administrative skills and leaned heavily on his wife whom I'll dub "Mrs. Bishop," to keep things going in the church without crossing swords with the Junta. I was shocked at his dismissal of my brother priest and I decided to speak to the issue in simple terms so that the bishop wouldn't miss my point. I began,

"So, Bishop, I'm sure we were both taught as children about the ledger in heaven where our deeds are cataloged and recorded, the good ones in gold and the rest in black ink. **What color ink** was used to record Fr. Dan's membership in Amnesty International in your opinion?"

"Probably gold," he mumbled.

"Did you consider that when you made your decision to expel Fr. Dan?"

"Don't lecture your bishop!" he shouted.

"My bad. I wasn't addressing you as a bishop but as a fellow Christian. **Your turn!**"

True discipleship consists in choosing Jesus unconditionally and without second thoughts, Jesus "uber alles" (Luke 9:51-62) (Luke 14:25-34). You cannot serve two masters, says the Lord. Existential choices are always either/or, there is no middle ground, says Kierkegaard. Like it or not, "You gotta serve somebody. It may be the devil or it may be the Lord, but you gotta serve somebody." (Bob Dylan)

Just an aside, when my contract came up for renewal after three years, the Bishop was **anxious to renew it** but not for the reason you may think. He had been paid my salary in dollars from the USA all that time while I was being paid in pesos which steadily devalued such that by the end of my tour I had lost 70% of my disposable income. As luck would have it, I had just become the father of my firstborn child, my son, Joey, and I needed more money for my growing family. So, I told Argentina not to cry for me and bequeathed my sizable personal library of theological and philosophical books to native clergy. (The usual parting gift from foreign missionaries serving in poor countries.)

Back to the war in the Southern Cone!

As the Malvinas/Falkland Island War raged on, the under-equipped Argentine forces froze their mittens off in Patagonia. They were no match for the British combat helicopters equipped with night scopes. Some of my students at I.S.E.D.E.T (an ecumenical school of theology in Buenos Aires that awarded Doctorates in three areas of study) left to join the fight.

With some extra time on my hands, I bought a ticket to see a return performance of a revolutionary folk singer **Mercedes Sosa** (Latin America's answer to Joan Baez), who had been in exile for six years. The theater was packed to the rafters. The crowd whistled and stamped their feet when she didn't appear on stage for forty minutes and they shouted, "Where is the lady-in-the -red dress?" The M.C. grabbed the mike and yelled, "I thought you were Argentines. Am I wrong? Real Argentines wouldn't demand an activist like Mercedes Sosa to submit to British **punctuality**?" The room went silent. People were shocked and hurt at being likened to the hated British who were killing their young men in Patagonia. Ten minutes later, when the concert officially began (_on time_ by normal **Argentine** standards), this artist showed that her comeback was worth the wait. She was truly a tonic for a people brutalized first by their own Military and now by the British. They needed to hear a song like, "Quand tengo la tierra," loosely translated as "When I get back my country." She was a petite (4'6"), cultural icon. A Baez and Dylan combo wrapped in a red skirt and shawl. If the energy in the room could be weaponized it might have won them the war. I felt blessed and privileged to be there and share the moment.

Judged by a jury of my peers (1983)

In addition to my academic duties in Buenos Aires, I decided to take classes in **Psychodrama** with local pastors of an Evangelist church. I will never forget the day when the announcement came to our group that the military junta was overthrown. You can't imagine the group's excitement. The psychodrama director asked the class to take their places on the stage's carpet and strike celebratory poses in **a victory tableau.** At first, I didn't join them. It wasn't my country that was liberated. Then, I got an idea. I could play the role of all the other countries who still had their hooks in Argentina. So, I got up, grabbed the edge of the carpet, and pulled it, toppling the statues. It was spontaneous and theoretically defensible but the others didn't think so. They returned to type and I found myself under a pile of screaming Argentines before I could groan **"Ooch!"** The director peeled them off me, attended to my rug burns and bruises, and invited the group to share. I trusted he meant verbally but I was open to all options. "Losers! You've taken the play out of role play, you idiots." During the sharing portion, while I was getting first aid, they told me that they had resented me from the first day I joined the group (so much for Christian fellowship) because I was North American. I was a part of that "first world" that had been robbing them of natural resources and selling them manufactured products at exaggerated markups stifling their industries that couldn't match the U.S. in quality or marketing. **My America,** according to them, was **a gang of international pirates** whose flag was the dollar bill. Wow! I had been comfortable living in the bubble of "White Privilege" and never would have imagined that I would not be welcomed anywhere in the civilized world. All this time, I never really took to heart or got the message that the **Marxist theology at I.S.E.D.E.T.** (the school where I taught) espoused. I never saw myself as one of those Yankee Doodles that was Doodling the Third World. I had assumed the irony of the Phil Oaks lyric, "Love me. Love me. Love me. I'm a liberal, "was written to burlesqued others, not little old me. Horizon, Horizons, Horizons. Thank you, Gadamer, for your analysis showing that Horizons are all we know and sometimes, all we choose to know. Anyone who wants to honor the past, should revisit it, reclaim it, re-evaluate, and refurbish it (De Lubac), instead of preserving it unchanged as the English did in the days of the Empire. Back then, regardless as to whether they were stationed in India, China, Africa, etc., the English maintained their identity by ordering umbrellas, Bola hats, and novels from London and measuring the world in inches, feet, and pounds instead of metric units. They are still fighting a battle over what it means to be English after Brexit.

Several months later, with newly opened eyes, I was able to recognize the myopia of a fellow Anglican missionary, who visited our group. She was an **English lady, a missionary stationed in Cordoba**. A group member asked her how she incorporated the art and customs of the indigenous people into the Anglican liturgy and she shocked us by claiming that the natives had no culture to speak of. I grabbed the mike and addressed this imperialist pastor. "Pastor, are you saying that before the English came, these people didn't celebrate harvest or weddings or funerals, etc., nor created artifacts, danced no dances, and sang no songs?"

"Nothing significant," she replied. "They're simple people." Right on cue, the director of the psychodrama group started **passing around tribal artifacts** made by these indigenous people. They were highly erotic and would have provoked reactions from anyone who had not been wearing a cultural blindfold for the past 13 years like this lady. As these objects made the rounds a phallic-shaped pipe landed in the pastor's hands. Daintily, she put it to her lips and the group exploded. Freud himself would have blushed at the incongruity, out of deference, we let the moment pass without comment and let her return clueless to her hotel to puzzle over some old chestnut like to Elger's Enigma Variations **for the 100th time** and cultivate **more civilized** pipe dream, far removed from those silly Latino students, miles away from parsing John Donne's erotic poem, "The Flea," or understanding the implications of his advice to missionaries bound for the Americas to take off their shoes when they land, "For the ground you tread on is sacred." "Horizons, horizons, horizons. Peace to you, my Anglican colleague. Sweet dreams. Sleep tight. Don't let the fleas bite."

After I read Pablo Freire's book, "**The Pedagogy of the Oppressed**" in Social Work school, I finally had categories to understand the cultural imperialism embedded in the mission work that took place in the American South West and still is active worldwide. Freire asserted that Spanish missionaries **treated native** Americans **like empty piggy banks** and inserted Spanish doubloons (Culture currency) in the slits atop their heads after shaking out whatever native coins they once harbored. In all, I came away from Italy richer with a new language to keep, a new appreciation for my Italian heritage, and a theatre upon which to rehearse ministry. After that, from my stint in Argentina, I received another language to treasure, a new self-awareness, and the insight into how that geopolitical machination (**cultural imperialism**) might be hiding consciously or not, up a Freire's sleeve.

*****

Part V

Back in the States

With a new tool!

Psychodrama – Lights, Candor, Action!

I know of an instance where philosophy segued seamlessly into practice, namely, the one I saw and trained for when I was a missionary in Argentina – Psychodrama. My trainer had studied theology in Switzerland (Balthasar's country) and learned psychodrama at the Moreno Institute in Beacon, New York (My country). Now, you may say, "Wait just a minute," less you accuse me of switching gears by praising Balthasar and then doing a 180 now by touting Psychodrama. Well, folks, there is a **common thread in both approaches, DRAMA.** Balthasar uses drama and drama history to flesh out his narrative theology and explains the ongoing workings of the Trinity in history as only drama can, For Balthasar, Drama is a didactic tool for dogma whereas Psychodrama uses DRAMA as a therapeutic tool in real-time, designed to raise consciousness and promote growth. Psychodrama is a group therapy that uses theater, improv, and to some degree projection and hypnosis to promote growth and mental health. It encompasses the personal and interpersonal realms, instructs by role-play and spontaneous interaction, draws upon conscious and unconscious reserves, unshaken repressed feelings and painful histories, uncovers the gallery of images that hide behind our words, and offers insights, existential choices, and group support to participants. But, most of all, it is the byproduct of Martin Buber's research **into mysticism** that generated his philosophical breakthrough namely the I – Thou relationship. His research led his colleague the psychiatrist Jacob Moreno to translate his findings into the therapeutic form known as psychodrama. **Balthasar borrowed Martin Bubers's idea** in his volumes on Theo-drama since the radiance of the Divine Form was also a call to action. I used psychodrama to teach bible studies in Buenos Aires (attracting university students to my classes from as far as 60k away) and I employed it successfully in teaching High

School Health classes in the NYC school system and my parishes in the States. (Truth be known, parishes prove to be the hardest sell of all!)

Pastoring Pastors

When I returned to the States as an Episcopal priest of the Diocese of Rockville Center, Long Island, I was asked if I was willing **to staff** a small colonial church across from a college and provide services on Sundays and staff the office two evenings a week. The church had a rectory and a congregation of 30 and dated back to **the 1740s as a plantation chapel with a slave gallery** and all. It had a few nice features – old gravestones and a white picket fence. One of the tombstones was over the grave of a 4-year-old who died in 1812 and at the base of her stone was chiseled the alphabet. I asked the local historian if this was customary and he said it was for a child's grave, "but usually the alphabet was buried below the ground for the child's eyes alone. Wouldn't want to send the kids to heaven illiterate." I guess there's no escaping homework on this side of the grave, nor the Book of Common Prayer on the other side – at least not for Junior Episcopalians.

One late Sunday afternoon, **I was visited by 12 of my full-time clergy brothers** and I gave them the grand tour. The sheen wore off when we entered the parish house that I rented to a therapist, an Irish woman who decorated it with a fountain, Irish harps, and crystal displays to make it less clinical. One of the clergies was aghast.

"New Age junk should have no place in a parish house."

"Calm yourself, sir," I said, "It's only furniture. This is an excellent outpatient drug and alcohol clinic and our parish 'cash cow'." He wasn't buying it.

Act I – the director sets the scene

So, I took him by the arm over to the church, and standing next to him near the pulpit we stared at the empty pews. Having placed him "on stage," having "set the scene," I was ready to begin the play.

"I understand your reaction to the decor of our clinic. The director designed it neither to appear as a hospital nor an Ethan Allen showroom but as a colorful and inviting ambiance for her clients. It is neither feng shui nor new age. It's just quirky and different. This building, I feel, is the opposite. It is not comfortable or inviting. Tall people cannot fit in the tiny 18th century pews and they are forced to ride them sitting side saddling during Mass. The main door cannot accommodate today's coffins so we have to place the dead upright outside so they can attend their funeral looking through that window. The glass is original and wavy and I'm sure the dead enjoy this historical touch. But, the thing that irks me most when I face my congregation is to see that **slave gallery hanging over their pious heads** like a **colonial crown of thorns** and I wonder how they can pray under such an atrocity. This is a historical building but it violates my idea of a church on so many levels, at least two architecturally, and I doubt whether the vestry or the state would let me tear the gallery down. So, I put up with it and see that part of my mission is to educate the children out of the cobwebs of the past and into the Lord's new age. Sorry, did I say New Age? In any case, I think there is more in the Bible, as I read it, against slavery than against furniture. And so, if you'd like to argue the point, have at it, I bet I win. Still, if your parish problems ever get you down as mine do me at times, and you start tipping a bottle of Southern Comfort daily just to take the edge off, come back and see us. **My clinic is your clinic**. Have a nice day."

Act II – warm up the remaining group for the drama

I rejoined the remaining eleven priests - 10 males, 1 female – and I grabbed a bagel and cream cheese while I explained psychodrama to the group.

"Today, we will create some statuary and see what they tell us. For example: (I struck a pose of Rodin's 'Thinker').

"What's this a statue of?"

"Rodin's Thinker."

"Who can make me a statue of friendship? I'll need two volunteers."

So far so good. Then I asked them to define prayer and they went around the room in turns. The consensus was that prayer was conversing with God.

"Who can make me a statue of a worshiper and God that demonstrates this conversation?"

A male priest volunteered and picked the female to play God. My instruction was to create a tableau without words. Just a configuration of actors in the act of praying to show the images behind and beyond the word in the dictionary. The male priest was the type who liked to be **large and in charge** and he jumped at the opportunity. First, he configured God, the female, as standing with her arms extended in front of her in supplication while he faced her, his arms extended outward like two wings from his body, head tilted upward at 90° and his gaze fixed on a point two feet above God's head. Very odd. **I asked them to converse** but they found it **impossible to do without eye contact.**

Then, I asked him to adjust the pose to include the meeting of eyes and then to switch from statue one to statue two. What was obvious to the group eventually dawned on him. And with the light bulb came the tears. He had prayed and led prayer groups for 30 years and never felt a connection with God, his interlocutor.

"I never realized this before," he said

"What you do in this rehearsal space," I told him, "You can replicate in the real world."

Then I made him reproduce his original statue and then slowly transition to the better one, three times. Back and forth. Back and forth.

"Tonight, my friend, you will know what to pray for – what God was waiting for you to ask Him in prayer. **'Lord that I may see.'"**

"Go in peace."

"Next!"

"My words fly up, my thoughts remain below; words without thoughts, never to heaven go." (Shakespeare).

******

Sharing

Not surprisingly, no more volunteer artists came forth to entertain us that day, and remained locked in the belief that 'Once is the definition of enough!' as was in the case of Jesus' exorcism in Mark 5:1-19, when the crowd preferred to keep their demons and bid Jesus Adieu (or a 'Don't, please don't come back. Come back.') thank you very much! So, I took my Aladdin's lamp off the auction block with a sigh and replaced it in its satchel. SHADE! Psychodrama was a new tool for me back then but today, as a seasoned therapist, I wouldn't be so heavy-handed but adopt Emily's pedological tolerance:

Tell all the truth but tell it slant – (E. Dickinson)

Success in Circuit lies

Too bright for our infirm Delight

The Truth's superb surprise

As Lightning to the Children eased

With explanation kind

The Truth must dazzle gradually

Or every man be blind.

Truth on a leash may be easy to preach. Truth in the raw with original claw should be handled by prophets who'd die for the cause!

In a Biblical Psychodrama on the Nicodemus pericope (after we playfully renamed him Nicotine mus, the chain-smoking rabbi), this sophisticated group of university students staged his encounter with Jesus in the setting of a cave similar to the ones the Essenes inhabited outside the city, one with a customary narrow-neck entrance opening up to a spacious room where Jesus and his disciples were gathered by a fire, their shadows displayed on the walls as in Plato's famous cave. Then the unforeseen happened in the session when Nicotine mus stood before these cave renters and heard Jesus claim that unless a man be born again, he cannot enter the kingdom of heaven and then be rebuked by the Lord. "And you a doctor of the law don't know this?" Nicotine mus tried to justify himself by asking Him sarcastically, "Can a grown man re-enter his mother's womb and be born again? "Bidababidaboom!" A light bulb came on for one of the members of the group sharp enough to spot the dramatic irony pregnant in the scene and started laughing. "My friend, THAT miracle just took place a minute ago when you imitated squeezing through the neck of this cave and positioned yourself to exit as a newborn in Christ. Happy Birthday to you."

Next

Flesh out Jesus' Lament and frustration with Jerusalem by adapting and staging Lewis Carroll's poem – Bessie's song 'To Her Doll,' psychodramatically and substitute God for Bessie and Israel for the doll named Matilda Jane. And you'll get a plaintive **new** reading of the text —

Matilda Jane, you never look at any toy or picture book

I show you pretty things in vain, you must be blind Matilda Jane

I ask you riddles and tell you tales but all our conversation fails

You never answer me again, I fear you're dumb, Matilda Jane

Matilda, darling, when I call You never seem to hear at all,

I shout with all my might and main but you're so deaf, Matilda Jane

Matilda Jane, you needn't mind, for though you're **deaf and dumb and blind**

There's someone who loves you, it is plain and that is Me, Matilda Jane. (What do you think? Try it on for size).

Part V
Theory

Theory
(Some in-depth reflections for anyone interested)
Gadamer's Hermeneutics-Mission tool #1
Interpreting Cultures

When **St. Augustine** wrote the first Western autobiography in the fourth century, he wasn't creating a scrapbook or album for posterity. He was writing a theological work to document pivotal moments leading to his conversion and give evidence of God's unrequited love and persistence in courting him which eventually brought him to the faith, turned him into a Latin Father of the Church, and showed him that his heart was destined for God. The Confessions was more than a biography. It was a document about Divine Providence and Conversion.

This book attempts to do the same, i.e., to be **more than a scrapbook of seminary life** in Rome in the late 60s, but **a bio-essay on the mission** of the church from the point of view of a priest-in-training and the thinkers who helped us make sense of the experience. If you're afraid of getting lost among the theological weeds and jargon that follow, you might check out a simplified version of Gadamer by Michael Sugrue on YouTube and Bishop Barron's treatment of Balthasar also on YouTube. I'd hate you to miss these gems.

Philosophy

For philosophers, life is a huge jigsaw puzzle (not a Whitman sampler), a box of puzzle pieces with no picture on the box lid to tell us what it depicts or how it will look when all the parts are meshed and accounted for. Philosophers hope that when completed, the puzzle would illustrate: the world's composition, the meaning of life, pivotal values, our place in the universe, who moves the levers of order or chaos (the Gods, for instance) and what is praiseworthy behavior and the ideal social order.

Philosophy calls for "global answers to life's intriguing questions" (as Garrison Keillor put it). Philosophy happens (according to Gadamer) when a thinker encounters an experience or question, something strange, startling, and disorienting that defies ordinary categories of explanation, stops him/her in their tracks, and demands a new answer. Plato says when this happens, it causes WONDER. The Greek word for such a show stopper is "Atopon," which literally means "out of place" a Renegade puzzle piece that doesn't seem to belong with the other pieces and calls for a new and grander puzzle. (From Gadamer's interview on YouTube, 1970.)

The job of a philosopher is to expand the horizon of understanding to make room for apparent anomalies, re-consider the border pieces, and expand the parameters to form a bigger picture that might accommodate these new elements. Sounds elitist but it's not! Huckleberry Finn and Jim had a philosophical moment floating on a raft on the Mississippi, looking at the stars, and started theorizing why there were so many. David Hume had such a moment when he questioned the belief in causality as an unfounded assumption. He said that when people see a white billiard ball hit a colored ball and make it move, they assume that the white one caused the other to move. What they witnessed, Hume claims, was only a succession of events; white ball rolls and touches the other and the other starts moving on its own. No causation; only one event following another. That's all. This didn't please scientists then or now whose findings assume causal connections.

When it came to trying to make sense of and discover some common threads woven into my overseas adventures. I needed a tool to interpret them, as well as a strategy as to where to begin. The obvious place to start is by connecting the frame, and puzzle pieces first if my analogy holds true. Fortunately, I discovered a philosopher whose forte was an interpretation of texts and culture. Leaving aside the objective pole of subject-object relationship for science to play with, Gadamer tried to discover the rules that govern the fuzzier fields of human intellectual activities such as history, art, literature, etc. anything that can't be reduced to a mathematical formula but which still deserves the name of knowledge. I modestly anticipated his theories in my Infamous Article where I also questioned as untenable the claim of philosopher Wilhelm

Dilthey who believed that to decode a text, all one had to do is forget your biases and examine it critically and dispassionately. In doing so he believed we may actually understand the text better than its author! "Bologna!" says Gadamer! I agree. Understanding (Horizons) comes from an interchange of opinions only after we each have a firm grasp of the other person's presuppositions and the world views that ground them.

*****

Passaggio

A word to the reader: Some readers enjoy biographies and are primarily interested in getting a sense of the historical times and settings under consideration, a cache of lived vignettes, a summary of the changes produced by the author/ traveler, lessons he learned, etc. If so, you can skip to part VI and rejoin the narrative of my metamorphosis. That being said, I suspect that there are others who, having followed my story thus far, and having been exposed to philosophical electives in the past may also be curious about the theological and philosophical insights I gained through traveling. Some people in this cast are very focused and austere. They have been known to purchase "trail mix" and discard the M&M's. They may accuse me of lowering the intellectual bar by leaving no pun or nun unturned in the course of this text. I can imagine them whining, "Give us more than a PowerPoint and slide show. We want to gnaw on the very nuts and currants of great thinkers with no sugar added, if you please."

Well, if that's your druthers, read on and see how Gadamer opened my mind to multiculturalism and how Balthasar made salvation history "nothing short of symphonic." Bon appetit!

Nonetheless, I refuse to completely surrender! I have opted to mix in <u>some</u> nonpareil chocolates (in the form of parentheses and asides) to gratify my tapeworm's sweet tooth and give into my own ADHD) As a result, you won't be treated to a Wagnerian Gesamtkunstwerk in this presentation, but I'll gladly serve up some Humperdinck and Gluck for luck.

Lament for non-philosophical theologians

"Little snail, dreaming you go weather and rose is all you know. Weather and rose Is all you see, drinking the dewdrop's mystery." (Langston Hughes)

The relationship of philosophy to Theology

Tertullian, a theologian of the third century, (OK, I didn't mention him above) was famous for brashly denying that reason or philosophy had anything to do with Faith. He proclaimed loud and clear, "Credo absurdum est," which means "I <u>believe because it is absurd</u>," or a variant citation of Tertullian is offered by James Moffatt, "Credible est, quia ineptum est." "I believe it because you couldn't just make this stuff up." Or, to put it another way, <u>"What has Athens (philosophy) to do with Jerusalem (faith)?"</u> The theologians I will quote would disagree with Tertullian. They would say that as rational human beings, we are obliged at least to attempt to understand our faith.

Gadamer's Philosophy

Your ideas and prejudices, in other words, the pieces you know, are a good starting point in the business of interpretation called hermeneutics. One must start from the familiar. Otherwise, it would be like asking a grown feral kid what language he/she wanted to learn. You have to own a language to acquire a new one and do it before the biological clock chimes 'sunrise,' say the scientists. Gadamer also suggests you have to be someone to meet and understand someone else through dialogue which involves you asking a question and getting an answer then based on that answer, you refine your question and go back and forth until your interlocutor says, "You got it," and in return. **as Cher would phrase** it **"I got you, babe,"** too. Gadamer modifies the old binary model of knowing i.e. (subject-object) dear to the empiricists into a more dialectical model i.e. subject-object-subject, that is a meeting of persons who talk about some topic each from their unique perspective until they can arrive at the same page about the matters at hand. Psychologists say that a baby's first conversation is wordless, consisting of smiles and nods which end in bonding and language. **Getting to a lingua franca is essential!** Complete agreement may be a long shot but worth the effort. Gadamer says that a lack of understanding across the globe comes from imposing one's opinions instead of starting with empathy. He says that this is one of the roots of the violence and wars we witness in the world today. Understanding comes from blending Horizons or as **Bob Dylan** put it, **"I'll let you into my dreams if you let me in yours."**

Needless to say, **Gadamer's approach collided with my Traditionalist Catholic background** where truth was one, unalterable, non-negotiable, and exclusively ours. But Gadamer's position coincides nicely with Vatican II's view that there exists a hierarchy of truths contained in the tradition, some more important and central than others. Truth be told, Gadamer's **championing of dialogue** over cultural imperialism resonates powerfully with my experience of acculturation in Rome which I featured in **my article**.

Gadamer's Philosophical Hermeneutics

To organize and draw lessons and conclusions from our stint in Rome, Tom and I needed some philosophical scaffolding, some overarching matrix to structure what we learned. I immediately recommended **Hermeneutics as the best choice.**

Why Gadamer's method? Because this was the philosophical tool I stumbled upon myself (on a modest scale), and described in **my article, "Symbolic Sinning,"** based on my experience in Rome, a viewpoint that nearly got me expelled and which the administration at NAC labeled "ridiculous." Let's just say, I have a personal stake in peddling hermeneutics.

When I took my walk of shame to Josef Fuchs' office, he told me that he had shown my article to a German colleague in the philosophy department who gave it a thumbs up. **I didn't know anything about Gadamer at the time**. His work was not published in English until 1975. But it has circulated in German since 1960 and I suspect that the professor of philosophy recognized some of Gadamer's ideas in my article.

What is 'Hermeneutics?'

Hermeneutics is the art or science of interpretation. The word comes from the deity Hermes, the fleet-footed messenger of the Greek gods and the patron of travelers, robbers, and interpreters. (We played all three roles on our Russian trip if you remember). The art of interpreting is an attempt to understand a text by knowing what the text means, then and now. **All three of the great monotheistic religions had hermeneutic commentaries for their sacred text.** The Hebrews had midrash for the Torah, the Muslims had Sunnah (tradition) and Hadith (saying of the Mohammad to illuminate the Koran) and Christians had the Church Fathers like Origin for the Bible. Origen was the first Christian commentator on a book of the Bible and also offered three ways to read a biblical passage.

When Luther proposed the Bible as the only authority (sola scriptura), he disputed the Roman Catholic teaching that revelation combines two sources: Scripture and Authoritative Tradition (hermeneutic). He then translated the Bible into the vernacular (in this instance German) so that everyone had a copy to read and decipher as they pleased.

Hermeneutics strives to obtain a message but not always the original message of the author. After ten years of marriage, you probably read an old love letter differently than before. Sorry, originalists.

Let me introduce **Gadame**r in a few quotes and key ideas he borrowed from other authors. **(Essential) Read slowly, and garner one insight at a time.**

1.   On the importance of language, "The limits of my language mean the limits of my world." Wittgenstein.

2.   On the development of dogma, "In a higher world it is otherwise, but here below to live is to change, and to be perfect is to have changed often." John Cardinal Newman.

3.   On interpretation, "Whenever men can form no idea of distant and unknown things, they judge them by what is familiar and at hand." Vico on Hermeneutics.

4.   Horizon - The totality of all that can be realized or thought about by a person at a given time in history and in a given culture. Gadamer.

5.   Dialogue - From Plato Gadamer discerns the centrality of dialogue as how we come to understand. Dialogue is rooted in and committed to furthering our common bond with one another to the extent that it affirms the finite nature of our human knowledge and invites us to remain open to one another.

6.   On time-Heidegger's idea of "Dasein" of being in the world means I am a prisoner of the moment. The past is restrictive and has to be revisited and re-incorporated with the present. (c.f.de Lubac) Are you still with me? Living in time is like riding a conveyor belt. Bye, bye, past.

Definitions:(essential)

Fusion of Horizons: People come from different backgrounds and it is not always possible to remove oneself from one's history, culture, gender, or language and enter an entirely different system of attitudes, beliefs, and ways of thinking. If I want to understand meanings, I must venture beyond the domain of the physical sciences and approach my subject with who I am, where I come from, and what I know, and then I conduct a Q&A in the style of Socrates or Detective Columbo. If after that dialogue, real understanding still eludes me, I revisit the subject again and again until it becomes clear, transparent, and acquired. This allows me to break out of my shell and become a new creature, blended and bigger, an American Yankee and son of Italy combined.

Pronesis (Aristotle's practical wisdom) emphasizes our being in the world as opposed to merely having a theoretical apprehension of it. Pronesis is a mode of **insight into our concrete situation**, a mode of insight that has its rationality, irreducible to a set of rules. It cannot be arrived at by mere thinking and is completely oriented to the case at hand.

Note: Besides the foregoing summaries, you can find excellent lectures on Gadamer on YouTube by Prof. Michael Sugrue. Worth checking out! YouTube History of Philosophy by Arthur Holmes Wheaton, College professor.

Finding the proper frame that fits the puzzle (application))
(1982 Argentina)

Now that you know something of Gadamer's **concept of "horizon,"** let me jump the gun by showing how I managed to shift the horizon of a Presbyterian congregation from a verbal redaction (story) to the visual depiction (the stain-glass window) while taking their parsimony into account (to save postage).

Side trip - Argentina (1970)

We are now in the 80's in Argentina where I served as an Anglican missionary to both Anglican and Presbyterian congregations. The Presbyterians were on the verge of sending a letter to Scotland to settle this question, i.e. "Is the bible the word of God or just a book containing the word of God?" This was a problem of hermeneutics: Should they stick with their Church's traditional definition of the **Bible as the word of God** or adopt a more enlightened one? I told them to save the stamp and look at the stained-glass window behind the high altar. The window depicted the scribes showing the Scrolls of Scripture to Herod and the Magi. "Where would you say the living word of God was that day? 1) Only in those dusty scrolls of scribes, or 2) Squirming and kicking across town while getting his diapers changed?" The question broadened their horizon and led to some interesting thinking about how "God is a God of the Living" and not a prisoner of pen and paper or parchment and quill. "Copy that," says the mathematician/philosopher Blaise Pascal. After he had a personal revelation experience that redirected him away from philosophical speculation and back to the Bible and to the God of the Bible, a living God – the God of Abraham, Isaac, and Jacob, and us.

"Doctrine exists in the play of lively minds." John Henry Newman

Gabriel Moran, who worked on the Vatican II documents and the New Catechism had a nice way of defining **revelation as when** "the invisible God from the fullness of his love, addresses men as his friends and moves among them to invite and receive them into his own company. The proper response to such revelation is belief, hope, and love." That's very personal. Cardinal Newman contrasts this personal touch of God which speaks to the inner man over and against faith understood as merely consenting to a collection of dry dogma, propositional formulations, and decrees. He writes, **"Persons influence us, voices melt us, looks subdue us, deeds inflame us. No man will be a martyr for a conclusion. Nor should he be."** If the "handing on" (tradition) is soulless and antiseptic, how can it demand consent? Should the faith be so thematized and over-analyzed (theologized to death) as to relegate it to academia?" Clearly not!

Horizons -Frames for Understanding Cultures & Epochs

Before I got to Rome, I thought the films of **Federico Fellini** were contrived, exaggerated, and bizarre - the stuff of side shows, ersatz, unreal, even though they were shot on location and used real people alongside actors (Neo-Realism). **Fellini claimed, "Il visionario è l'unico realista."** (The visionary is the only realist). How indeed would a foreigner who never attended Opera Buffa, laughed at Punch and Judy Show, or attended Carnival understand him or his vision. But once viewed from the vantage point of the seven hills and heard in their original colloquial Italian, his films are as much a slice of life as una fetta di pizza. Friends, trust me, even opera sounds believable in Italian. It's all a question of horizons.

Closer to home, I always thought that my Italian grandmother's opinions and **stereotypes** (i.e. **Germans are smart but they're crazy** and Japanese are tricky but you wouldn't want them as enemies) were verbal shrapnel from WWII propaganda bombs. What a surprise to find the same ideas still flourishing in the 60s in the poorer and old parts of Borgo Pio and Borgo Angelico, and I even found a portrait of Mussolini framed in the back room of a religious article store in St. Peter's Square. The sun never sets on some horizons.

As I told my friend Ken, the amateur photographer, to get the picture right, it's not enough to aim the camera; you've got to have the right settings. Take, for example, Mike, one of **our classmate**s involved in our outreach. He **was Italian on both sides** of the family. Still, we couldn't understand why he played by different rules than the rest of us Americans. Our bad! We saw him as a fellow American and so we didn't get why he acted as such a controlling Son of Bologna with us his peers. "Who died and made him Capo?" we asked ourselves. My grandmother would have pegged him in a second, "Sicilian!" and she would have been right. Guess we should have paid more attention to Scorsese movies when judging this classmate. As they say in Cinecitta, the Roman equivalent of Hollywood if you "De Sica you will finda (la faccia brutta) villainy in unlikely places." Sorry, Nonna (grandma) and Federico. Avevano ragione, as Sofia Loren says. Wait! Never mind! Does a perfect statue like Sophia have to talk to? NO! Nor act, for that matter.

Last on the horizon. When I arrived home from Italy after four years, I was greeted at the airport by my mom and Cousin Willy, (Guglielmo to his father). I confess I suffered a major cultural shock when he kissed me and proceeded to walk with me arm in arm. Ten hours earlier, at Fiumicino Airport in Italy, this would have been perfectly normal, but now that we're in America, I instinctively pulled back. Mi dispiace tanto, zio! Obviously, he thought I was Romanized and I thought of him as Americanized while the sun lingered tentatively above both horizons. Horizons in counterpoint. Consider how these seemingly "harmless" quips of Mark Twain would be received today in a polarized America: "God created war so that Americans can learn Geography" or "On the evolutionary scale, today's man is somewhere between an ape and a Frenchman." Caveat comicus. Back to Willy.

Over the years, **Cousin Willy** was a frequent guest at our house and after his wife passed he came to stay. He was my mother's half-brother and had worn many hats as a laborer in his day, e.g. as a seasonal worker at Coney Island Seaside Park, a butcher at a slaughterhouse, and finally as a machinist at the Brooklyn Navy Yard. His wife was an insanely jealous woman who would come to his jobs, cause a row, and force him to seek new employment. She was nuts! One time, she intentionally set herself on fire. Still, Willy undauntedly shouldered his cross.

You'd never guess from looking at him what kind of home life he endured. He used to follow her into the woods so that should she get lost, he could guide her back home. (they **lived in a cabin in the Catskills**). Willy had the aplomb of a well-shaven, Italian Santa with a full face, a bald pate, an upturned elfin nose, battle scars from Ethel, and weighing in at a solid 250 lbs. When I was born, he came to see me, his sister's first baby, and broke out laughing. "Look at the pointed head on that little guy, Daisy. Peculiar, just peculiar!" Needless to say, that comment made Willy a persona non grata for the next five years. Eventually, he was pardoned!

Willie - seen as "a gentleman from the old country"

I recall how whenever he told us stories, his eyes would dance, he salivated and leaned into the punch line. Such as, "When you see a well-dressed gentleman step out of his limousine in front of a ritzy hotel, with a scowl on his face, this isn't because of where he just came from or where he's going, it's from what he's stepped in." Occasionally, he'd share pearls such as, "Don't read the funny papers; they'll give you IDEAS!" That didn't make a lot of sense to me but what should one expect from a guy with the surname BIZZARO? Ask him any time night or day how he felt and he'd always say the same thing, BEAUTIFUL, broadcasting the word syllable by syllable through his several missing teeth. He was indeed a guileless, beautiful person. He had radiance (c.f. Baltazar). He never complained and never defamed anyone. He was a genial jolly soul, a devoted and faithful husband, and a great father to their two boys who turned out normal except for an occasional case of the "willies" (c.f. Billy Collins poem of that name). Lord knows, living with Ethel was a walk on the wild side. If, for example, he read "Jack and Jill" to his sons he would have to change the girl's name to Joe and if his wife looked over his shoulder and noticed the change, she would pitch a fit. "Why did you change the name? Who is Jill to you? What are you trying to hide?" Once she beaned him with a coffee pot (the Infamous "Coffee Beanngs (ibid), a respectable variant to the ballistic frying pan). Willy weathered the blow, moaning, "Good to the last drop." then left for stitches. Un Bel Di the following year, fates were determined to follow up on the coffee pot crown affair when a co-worker asked Willy to lend him his car to take the secretary out to "lunch." Fearing what the discovery of a stray hairpin could cost him, Willy refused at first but eventually gave in. When he got the car back, he inspected it meticulously and found nothing incriminating.

He picked up the little woman at her sister's in Brooklyn and they drove to their cabin in rural Upstate New York. The car was not air-conditioned, the windows were wide open, and gradually the highway and paved roads turned to dusty country ones. He could see Ethel casually fanning herself through the rearview mirror but then just behind her, clear as day, there appeared incontrovertibly the dainty bare footprints of the secretary **etch-a-sketched on the rear window by the dust of the road.** He hit the gas and welcomed her cursing, his recklessness which guaranteed that she was facing forward. With a single sweeping gesture, he stopped at their door, whisked her quickly inside fussing and cussing, and returned with his handkerchief to the scene of the crime. Willy's life was a happy mix of three elements: Rahner's supernatural existential (grace operative throughout the world as a trailer of the Beatific Vision) Baltazar's treatise on Transcendental Beauty (God's watermarks on history and creation and how Willy described how he felt) and last but not least, good old Brooklyn savoir-faire and Italian "Che me ne frega" nonchalance. That was Willy theologically speaking! Rahner writes "Have you ever been good to someone (like Ethel, Willie's wife) who didn't show the slightest sign of gratitude or comprehension and when we also were not rewarded by the feeling of having been selfless, decent, etc.? If we have had such an experience, we have experienced an 'eternal spirit' that is more than merely a part of this temporal world. We have 'taken the plunge' into the world of saints. (Rahner's Theological Investigations Vol. III) Willie is definitely on my list of bread-and-butter saints who don't get a feast day (C.F. Karl Rahner's book The Mystical Way in Everyday Life, formerly titled "Faith that Loves the World).

Willy as the Mad Hatter

Here's a Willy story I can't verify:

Willy said he once **worked at a men's hat factory.** Actually, the hats were produced at a different site and sprayed with a stiffening chemical to keep them from being crushed during shipping. Willy's factory had to remove the chemicals with a volatile solvent before shaping them into a market-ready product. Unfortunately, there was no suitable place to dump the spent mixture so they poured the waste into the toilet. A new man unfamiliar with this practice went into the bathroom smoking a cigar. Before leaving, he threw the glowing butt between his legs which propelled his butt off the bowl, through the air, and out of the stall. It was the best Fourth of July his co-workers had ever seen and they couldn't wait for another smoker to join the team.

What's your take on his story? Truth or trash or both? To me, this sounds like a vignette from NPR's news quiz, "Wait. Wait. Don't tell me." I'm sure Willy would have liked that show and maybe would submit some original vignettes of his own.

*****

The Forest Spoke

Mission Insight #2: The Kaleidoscope

I never saw a moor,

I never saw the sea,

Yet know I how the heather looks

And what a billow be

I never spoke to God

Nor visited in Heaven

Yet am I certain of the spot

As if a chart were given

Love is a many splendor thing like colorful shards

tumbling into new patterns as the world's tube turns

Faith as seeing

"Taste and see how good the Lord is"

The spiritual senses (Balthasar)

On the eve of his conversion, (after having vowed the year before to kill himself if he couldn't find an Absolute to believe in), the French philosopher Jacques Maritain, heard the trees in the forest whisper to him the word, **"Being"** (get it, existence transcendence as in Yahweh). Soon, thereafter, he heard lectures by Henri Bergson talk about the "elan vital."(the life force) and found what he had been looking for and became a Thomist philosopher. He wrote Art and Faith.

I believe the voice he heard, this theophany in the forest was the voice of the "forest primeval, the murmuring pines and the hemlocks 'trying to **Evangelize** him.' (That's what I think. **Wait! My** mind-chatter suggested two puns to share in the meantime 1) the name of the poem is **Evangeline** and 2) **For What It's Worth – The middle name of its author Henry WHAT IT'S WORTH Longfellow. (silly puns!)**

Phenomenology of E. Dickinson – a distiller of essences

Questions about the objectivity of beauty.

TRUTH

To hear an oreole sing;

may be a common thing,

or only a Divine.

It's not of the Bird

Who sings the same unheard

As unto Crowd

The fashion of the Ear

Attaireth that it hear

In Dun or fair

So, whether it be Rune

Or whether it be none

is of within

The Tune is in the Tree

The Skeptic showeth me

No, Sir! In Thy!

(Balthasar would say in both)

****

Real Theophanies vs Relics
Lucca (Birthplace of Puccini)

Once I became the proud owner of North American College's discarded Mercedes limousine in my third year in Rome, I drove a classmate to meet his family in Lucca. We sat in their kitchen discussing current events and talked about St. Gemma, their saintly relative who died in 1903. She had been given the stigmata before her First Communion and had to wear white gloves to hide the blood.

"She bore a lot of physical pain in her short life," said the lady of the house and went into gory detail. As if that was not enough to gross us out, she rose from the table, went over to a shelf, and returned to place an olive jar before us with an unknown content.

"Guess what these are?" she glowed.

"Beats me," I say.

"These are the gallstones of St Gemma," she beamed. I mustered the self-control not to curse in my best Romanache "porca la miseria! Que scifo" or vomit. I cringed to think what miraculous body parts might pass for olives in her pantry! **We didn't stay for lunch**. When it comes to relics, I'd sooner own a Stradivarius than the skull of John the Baptist or his receipt for roasting crickets.

Surprisingly, while I was in Rome, I heard of a priest who had the stigmata living 20 kilometers outside the city. Wild horses couldn't have dragged me there to see him. This might have been truly miraculous but who cares? What's the point? Who wants a bloody high five from a latter-day Padre Pio and winds up getting your pinky stuck in the palm of his hand? Maybe my brother would still be interested enough in investigating this modern stigma. For my part, I applaud the decision of Pope John XXIII who suspended the morbid practice of sacristans to unveil the skulls of saints at St Peter in Chains for the price of a few lire. My experience in a Luccan kitchen only confirmed my conviction that not every relic is inspiring, nor every religious practice is tasteful or relevant.

Purging your mind of relics

The lesson I took away from those Luccan gallstones was to inventory my Catholic background and decide what to keep as holy, essential, and useful for prayer and what to toss aside like pieces of a puzzle that I no longer own. The British sculptor, Antony Gormley, who in his twenties volunteered to help dip crippled believers into the miraculous waters of Lourdes, and after countless disappointments, he became so disgusted with the practice that he fled to India for an identity make-over (hoping it wasn't true that once a Catholic, always a Catholic). He took up Eastern meditation with a guru so as not to remain enslaved and branded as a cradle Catholic for life. Today, he's 'in recovery' as a celebrated sculptor in London. Check him out on YouTube.

*****

The story of Antony Gormley, an artist on the mend

He has an interesting history. As a child his aunt made him take a nap after lunch in a hot, dark small room. It terrified him until he stopped fighting it, closed his eyes, and discovered an infinite inner world with no boundaries, no objects, and no dimensions. He eventually began to feel cooler and more comfortable in that sweat-box of a room and to experience it as a place of freedom. After he came back from India as a Buddhist, having swapped **the cross** for a bohda **fig tree** (go figure), A la Siddhartha, Antony began a career of self-discovery and artistic proselytizing by **encasing himself** in plaster of Paris and then using these molds to make bronze statues of himself with eyes closed. "**I learn by making things as a conceptual artist.**" He placed his creations atop buildings, horizontally attached to walls and ceilings and shorelines, etc. to force onlookers to tap into their own experience of being in a body, which is to say an energy field encased in a skin locked in space and time. By letting others in on his Lazarus experience (reminiscent of being entombed by his aunt), **he hopes to take art out of museums and churches**, to save it from being like other objet d'art (more clutter in the world) and instead raise the question of the draw-backs of also being entrapped in <u>another prison,</u> namely the **secondary skin** called **Architecture**. Like Karl Rahner, Gormley is all about INTERIORITY.

Since we happen to be in Lucca, Italy. Let me share a bit of local color captured in a painting by a friend of mine **who studied in Lucca**. It is the omnipresent wraith of an elderly woman in widow's weeds, which either testifies how wonderful and irreplaceable Italian husbands are or simply acknowledges that the "mala fortuna" one encounters along life's milestones will dog you the rest of your life. There are many widows in Lucca.

Ad esempio a me piace vedere

For example, I fix on the sight

 La donna nel negro del lutto di siempre

of a figure in black by a doorpost at night

 Sulla la soglia tutte le sere

Woman in mourning; desperately yearning

 Che aspetta il marito che non torna mai

For a field-worker husband who's never returning

(From the Nicolo di Bari song, "For example ")

The question that beauty raises

Friends, let me pose this question: **What if beauty were more than just transient pleasure**, an ornamental trinket, or an innocent surprise? What if it were instead, an inchoate quality of all creation, tugging and directing our attention to look at the world more closely and finding therein the radiance of its roots, God's trademark, who is Being-in-Itself, who comes to lift us out of our myopia and confinement and broaden our vistas (Gadamer). If that be true, then every earthly thing God has made can be expected to exhibit in various degrees His Beauty, His Goodness, and His Truth, not in some disembodied Platonic way but found concretely and existentially in the finite creatures in this world and most fully in His holy incarnate Word. "God is the word that speaks himself." (Eckhart)

What if we stopped for a moment from seeing life pointillistically or piecemeal, i.e., labeling everything by category and stamping them as "nothing special" instead of recognizing them as "minor miracles" perishing at our door and prompting us to wonder why we hadn't noticed them before. (Dickinson). Suppose we could see His radiance beguiling us from every corner of creation and feel His pride in everything He made. If this seems too-goody-goody to take seriously, let me buy some credibility by citing the case of a classical pianist turned theologian, Hans Urs von Balthasar. At the age of five, Balthasar attended a performance of Schubert's Mass with his father and was so taken by its beauty that he begged his dad for piano lessons and was on track to becoming a classical pianist when, by chance, he attended a retreat and decided to abandon Schubert, sell his collection of Mozart symphonies and join the Jesuits. I guess you can say that he **grew up with Schubert but dedicated the rest of his days to Jesus.**

When I lived in Brooklyn, I heard of a groom who during the wedding rehearsal seemed distracted. He started looking about the church, greedily drank in the scripture readings word by word, then pivoted abruptly and walked out shouting, "I don't." He swapped the bride for an altar and became a priest. I have three questions about the break-up. First, did he ever regret that decision, second, does this only happen in Brooklyn, and finally, is he some kind of nut? As to that, only Balthasar, his ex, and God can opine.

Definition of Beauty

In defining beauty, **Balthasar follows St. Thomas Aquinas** who says that **beauty has three components: 1) Wholeness** or **Integrity**, 2) **Harmony** among its constituting elements plus a certain 3) **Radiance** which draws us closer to whisper its secrets. (Check out the black-and-white confusing picture on the following page and then turn the page to decipher what it is from a more traditional rendering of the subject. Suffice for now to point out that despite the revolutionary changes brought about by pioneers like Pablo Picasso and Braque, St. Thomas' criteria still basically hold true today (with a little fine-tuning).

But what about modern art like Picasso's?

The advancements in photography had threatened to put realistic 19th-century painting out of business, causing a horrified Pablo Picasso to declare, "It's over." In the crosshairs was art like that of the Hudson River School which tried to copy nature faithfully on huge canvases with a signature splash of golden light added to praise **nature over technology** (see painting). Fortunately, Picasso, a superb draftsman, decided not to throw in the towel although in his later works, he threw in the kitchen sink, some bull's heads, a guitar, and even extra eyes but never the towel. He reserved towels and sheet music for collages. Picasso made a monumental breakthrough when attempting to paint Gertrude Stein's portrait. To do justice to that commission, **Picasso borrowed from two sources**, the flat visage and dark eyes from the statue of the Virgin Mary which he saw in Gozo, Spain, and some exotic and geometry touches from African face masks and **voila**, he produced the angular representation of the face of his American patron, Gertrude **Stein. Gertrude told him the portrait didn't look like her and he replied, "IT WILL."** In the end, he succeeded in changing her eyes and ours forever. Horizons were stretched, culminating in the next breakthrough which was "Les Demoiselles d'Avignon," the first cubist painting.

Having said this, I would like at this point to introduce you to the rich and complex thought of Hans Urs von Balthasar and his aesthetical theology. I have tried to make his ideas a little more accessible through vignettes drawn from my own dabbling in the arts and my European travels, plus some photos to concretize terms like radiance, form gestalt, etc., and some selected verses of Emily Dickinson to add context and body.

Question: How can an **invisible** God be beautiful? "Elementary, Watson," said Holmes. "**Perhaps, He's as transparent and ubiquitous as Music!**" Then he picked up his violin and played Ascent of the Lark.

******

The Theology of Beauty
Balthasar

"Christ is the unchangeable valid blueprint for every situation in the world and in history" (Balthasar)

Intro: If you are reluctant to delve headlong into the twenty-volume work of a scholar like Balthasar (without having a philosophical background), don't panic, relax! I know of a beautiful film which illustrates a major tenet of his theology, that "love alone is credible."

When I was twelve years old, I saw a film on T.V. redolent with Balthasarian themes such as yoking the mundane and eternity through the couplings of art. The movie narrated how a down-on-his-luck landscape artist, after being told that his pictures lacked "soul,' meets a fey by chance in Central Park, a ten-year-old girl dressed in an old-fashioned outfit, who speaks of an event that happened long ago though they just happened. Every time our hero saw her, she appeared five years older and shyly confessed that she was rushing to grow up to be his wife and had her portrait painted. After two years and three more meetings, she reached her goal, full-grown and ready to be immortalized on canvas. By then, she succeeded in becoming his obsession, his passion, his inspiration and ours as well. Thanks to the director's deft storytelling, the usual boundaries which separate life and death, fantasy and reality, doubt and belief have crumbled and Debussy's impressionistic score (arabesque #1) gently draws us into Eben's garret to witness Jennie posing for her promised portrait. Jennie disappears and Eben frantically searches for clues to find her and finally rents a boat hoping to meet her where she was last seen years ago, Land's End Lighthouse. Once again, the director calls upon Debussy's wizardry, summoning storm clouds and a tidal wave bearing down in an effort to separate the couple. This piece of music is entitled "Dialogue between the Wind and the Waves," from Debussy's larger tone poem "La Mer." You might recall the term "dialogue" from our discussion of Gadamer's classic treatment of hermeneutics: Truth and Method.

By the end of the film, I was totally in love with Jennie Appleton (ending my crush on Shirley Temple and preparing the way for Sophia Loren). Nevertheless, it took 60 years plus Balthasar's brilliance and writing to unpack the theological gold-salting "Portrait of Jennie." We all know <u>from the catechism</u> that God made the world but before reading Balthasar, I never realized that He is only an arm's length away, near enough to <u>touch His robe</u> *through the vehicle of finite beauty* and begin a <u>real</u> relationship.

The director, Joseph H. August's use of atmospheric cinematography, impressionistic music, and a palette of black and white succeeds in pulling us away from the veneer of every day and into the magic of the story. By the end of the film, we find ourselves standing with a group of young people in a museum staring at the painting of Jennie Appleton now fully grown, portrayed in radiant Technicolour with a wee blush of eternity in her cheeks. That's a Balthasarian touch! Watch it on YouTube, "Portrait of Jennie."

*****

Form Suggested

I discover Balthasar

I never heard of Hans Urs von Balthasar while I was in seminary. There was no course on contemporary theology in our curriculum at the Greg and Baltasar wasn't one of the periti (scholars) at Vatican II where his name might have come to my attention. He was a theological outlier like myself. His degree wasn't in theology but in German Cultural Studies and music. As I said, he was sold on Music at the age of Five after hearing Schubert's Mass. However, while he was preparing for a career as a concert pianist, he attended an Ignatian Retreat and decided instead to become a Jesuit. That wise decision led to him becoming one of the greatest theologians of our times, on a par with his co-luminary Karl Rahner. Still, this choice had its drawbacks. As a novice, he had to endure the standard curriculum of scholastic theology (as I did at the Greg) which he found to be so dry and insipid, that he almost left the novitiate. Fortunately, the Order transferred him to Lyons, France where he met Pere de Lubac, a progressive patristic scholar, a member of the "back to the sources" movement whose approach to theology involved revisiting the writings of the early church fathers in the hopes of recovering from them an immediacy and freshness which had been fractionated out by centuries of pedantic scholastic distillations. Balthasar wrote, "The truth that is merely handed down without being thought anew from its very foundation has lost its vital power."

After completing his studies, Balthasar was offered several university chairs but chose instead to become a student chaplain and continue conducting Ignatian retreats. In the end, Balthasar left the Jesuit Order on good terms and he and Adrienne von Speyr, a medical doctor and mystic, founded a lay institute of their own as a venue to equip laymen to witness the faith in their life situations. In his book, "Christian Witness," Balthasar spells out their mission "to attempt to shape one's life in loving response to the trinitarian love of God and thus to place oneself at the disposal of Jesus' work of establishing God's Kingdom of love among men."

Same Form Revealed

As I said, he partnered with Adrienne von Speyr whose mystical visions he considered profound and authentic and whose ecstasies he transcribed and published. For his part, drawing upon his background in the arts, Balthasar crafted an aesthetical theology, comprising over twenty volumes grouped into three sections: "The Glory of the Lord (his treatise on Beauty), "Theodrama" (his treatise on the Good), and "Theologic" (a treatise on Truth). Students of philosophy will recognize these as the three classical Transcendental Qualities of Being, which is to say, that anything that exists can be said to be real and good and beautiful to some degree just by virtue of existing! We call these qualities Transcendentals because they go beyond particular labels and individual instances and share a commonality with their source, i.e., Being-in-itself, aka God. Unlike his secular predecessor, the philosopher Emmanuel Kant, Balthasar doesn't begin his trilogy with a "Critiques" of the Reason (Truth) as Kant did, but with a treatise on "The Beautiful," a wise choice in our postmodern world. Given that nowadays, if one chooses to begin with Truth or Ethics you may find yourself facing blow-back as fierce as the one you might expect trying to enforce mask mandates on airplanes during the pandemic. Furthermore, Balthasar asserts that beauty is every bit as objective as Truth and Goodness since all three are qualities of God and by extension are consequently present throughout creation.

Balthasar is not the first theologian to write on 'the beautiful.' There are treatments of beauty found in the writings of Origen, Bonaventure, Aquinas, etc., and the experience of beauty has been recognized in every epoch and clime across the world. Which of us hasn't been stopped dead in his tracks by something beautiful and then moved to tell the world? Guess what I saw, what I heard, what I felt?

Balthasar's theology starts "from the top," beginning with the concept of Doxa, the radiance of God which shines brightest in Christ, God's icon.

*****

Radiance in the forms
Beauty as a Wayside Shrine

As an artist, Balthasar focuses on the **concrete beings we observe in the world**. Such beings consist of two components: matter or potential to exist and an inchoate **"form"** or a **gestalt** – which unifies the matter it informs and invites us to notice it. Balthasar insists that the beauty we encounter in the world is not just an ornamental or accidental quality like tinsel on a tree but the gestalt, the form of a thing, (like a tree ity, so to speak) an organizing principle that shapes it, that pervades every limb, every evergreen needle and makes it recognizable as a tree and in its small way, a testimony to the **"kabod," the glory of its Maker**. **Chesterson says** that every artist knows that the **form is not superficial but fundamental**; that the form is the foundation. The sculptor knows that the form of a statue is not the outside of the statue but **inside the statue;** even, in the sense, inside the artist's imagination. This **"Kabod,"** this **radiance of God** is beautifully described in the book of Revelation: "He carried me in spirit to the top of a vast mountain and pointed out to me the city, the holy Jerusalem....radiant with the glory of God. Her brilliance sparkled like a precious Jewel." (c.f. The pictures of a fountain at dusk and Roman ruins by the Argentina painter Jose Ibera (which I included), appear illuminated with just such an undisclosed light source. Like art, **spiritual beauty is also perceived by our senses** when enabled by grace to behold both the gift and the giver, the tree and the untrimmed trimmer. When seen by faith, when one experiences creation as an encounter and not merely a fist full of sense impressions or Monads which Martin Buber would term, an "I-IT external relationship" as distinct to a real encounter which Buber terms an I-Thou relationship which is welcoming visitation.

This can be seen vividly in the Biblical passage about the woman with the hemorrhage who said, "If I touch the hem of His garment, I will be healed." Faith put her in touch with both his hem and power, making her gesture a genuine **encounter**. Beauty my friends, is but the hem of His garment, says Balthasar.

Theology as a <u>Prayer Response</u>

Great theology is prayerful. Balthasar says, "**The greatest tragedy in the history of Christianity** was neither the Crusades nor Reformation nor Inquisition but rather the split that separated theology and spirituality at the end of the Middle Ages." For Balthasar's Theology is not a dispassionate discipline (mere data) but an inquiry rehearsed "on its knees," one that grows and evolves from devote study as it did in the convents and monasteries of the early church before sacred theology became a study to be outsourced to Secular Universities. As an artist and retreat master, **Balthasar urges anyone engaged in doing theology to consult their hearts** and tap the inspiration of poets, psalmists, Christian mystics and life itself while plying their craft. "Lovers are the ones that know most about God. The theologian must listen to them." (Preface pg.12 from Love Alone is Credible, Von Balthasar) Here we find echoes of the advice St. Augustine gave when asked how to interpret St. John's Gospel. He replied, "Let a lover read this Gospel. He will understand it." From an excellent little book, "Key to Balthasar" by Aidan Nichols, let me offer a thumbnail sketch of his main ideas.

Balthasar's Main Ideas and Major Takeaways

(Key: Chapter I, my summary from the book, <u>Keys to</u> <u>Balthasar)</u>

1.   We grasp beauty through the senses and we can trust our senses. (realist epistemology)

2.   Where we find one of the transcendentals, the others are also present, i.e., where there is beauty, there is also truth and goodness.

3.   To understand is to accept what is given in experience as it offers itself to us.

4.   The universe shows itself to us apart from and beyond our subjective needs.

5.   **In the act of knowing, we receive more than we project.** (the richness and objectivity of experience) (as against Kant who claimed we will never know the object in itself).

6.   To exist is to be part of the network of being so that we do not see things as merely separate monads but as part of the cosmos as ubiquitous as the background noise left over from the Big Bang. The word "Universe" means turning towards the ONE

7.   We are aware of our finitude and see ourselves and every other finite being against the background of Infinity. (Rahner would agree)

Balthasar **respected** mysticism which Nietzsche mocked saying in, "The Gay Science (Sect 126), "Mystical explanations are thought to be profound: In fact, they aren't even superficial." (c.f. Michel Sugrue treatment of Nietzsche on YouTube).

****

Karl Rahner/Balthasar – two approaches, same mountain
(You may have to read the next three paragraphs three times to see the difference)

Balthasar's rival, Karl Rahner (who was my Pere de Lubac) is also a theologian grounded in the "Spiritual Exercises" of St. Ignatius and also had "calluses on his knees" from prayerful reflection but his approach is vastly different. Rahner's theology is a Christian anthropology in dialogue with Emmanuel Kant. Rahner addresses a different audience, uses different methods and builds upon different foundational ideas and sensibilities. **While Balthasar uses artistic experience** as a paradigm for understanding Revelation and the Incarnation and starts with the Bible, **Karl Rahner posits the "vorgriff," the pre-apprehension of being** by which every act of knowing implies and moves toward the Horizon of Truth, i.e., God, who is Truth Itself. Man hungers for God and ingests Him one truth at a time.

Balthasar's theology is a theology "from above," beginning with the mysteries of Creation, the Trinity and the Incarnation, and exacting from these dogmas **lessons for man to live by**. In contrast, Rahner's theology starts at ground zero as philosophical anthropology which attempts to establish the conditions for the possibility of belief for agnostics. His approach is more like Jacob's ladder, i.e. a climb to the top. But the two are not so far apart when it comes to Christology. In the second series of his Trilogy, Balthasar also engages in a "theology from below" and taps into his extensive knowledge of **drama** to show that Jesus' actions, His performance on the world stage, forcefully proclaim who He is and Who sent Him.

For Balthasar, art and Jesus call out to us. They are self-evident to any who have eyes to see and ears to hear. As Meister Eckhart said, "God is the word that speaks itself." Balthasar locates such words (messages) in the context of creation/incarnation. Like St. John's claims in his

Gospel, God calls us by name. His invitation is as personal and as tailored as Schubert's reply to music critics when they ask why he doesn't write happy music. Schubert answered with a question, "Is there any such thing as happy music?" Evidently, not in Shubert's WELT. Shubert had to follow his mournful muses for his music to be true, beautiful, and good and for his concerts to radiate the life force of his persona. God also has to follow His being as True, Good, and Beautiful to be Yahweh, **I AM** the creator.

✱✱✱✱✱

The mystical in the everyday

One final point, Balthasar has some <u>Good News for the laity</u>. **By acknowledging the fact that spiritual senses cohabit with the physical senses, he has democratized the mystical** as not **belonging exclusively to saints and apostles but open and welcoming to all who receive the Gospel** or follow the sirens of beauty to God. Then, for spiritually awakened souls like that of poet Gerard Manley Hopklins, this world literally crackles with God like aluminium foil.

Ok, one last word about Karl Rahner. Rahner taught that Non-Christians can in their basic orientation and fundamental option accept the saving grace of Christ unconsciously. Even some who formally reject Christ may actually be living through Him. Rahner calls them "Anonymous Christians."

Apologetics: Sharing the Message

This World is not Conclusion.

A Species stands beyond

Invisible, as Music

But positive, as Sound

It beckons, and it baffles

Philosophy, don't know

And through a Riddle, at the last

Sagacity, must go

To guess it, puzzles scholars

To gain it, Men have borne

Contempt of Generations

And Crucifixion, shown (c.f. Rahner's vorgriff)

Apologetics, according to St. Thomas, is the study of metaphysical truths we can arrive at through reason and syllogisms without recourse to special revelation. (e.g. St. Thomas' five rational proofs for the existence of God) and (Karl Rahner's Spirit in the World)

*****

Finale

Homage to Balthasar

Balthasar parses the scriptures and tradition like a musician might interpret a score by making connections and weaving themes while remaining faithful to the meaning of the texts. Through the lens of prayer and his research into the writings of Church Fathers, he gives the reader a spiritual and scholarly "command performance." What we have in his aesthetic theology is a virtuoso blend of dogma and insight which impels the reader to discern the objective light of the Creator throughout creation and human life through the inner dynamics of the Trinity operating in the life of Jesus who is the Father's incomparable gift. Balthasar lends us an artist's eyes. His holistic presentation unites the individual mysteries of the faith to produce a finished work, a cogent and compelling narrative. Balthasar tends to criticize contemporary theology, whether conservatory or more innovatory for failing to view creation and revelation sufficiently holistically. "The forms inherent in creation and revelation can only be grasped when creation and revelation are viewed as they were meant to be viewed, not as fragments but as a symphonic whole." **"Truth is Symphonic,"** is one of Balthasar's favorite expressions. (Key to Balthasar pg. 9) In other words, he does not dogmatically single out one melody line such as Incarnation, without adding a philosophical counterpoint like the phenomenological understanding of Man (as a being who learns who he is through his contact with the world and others) and an optimistic epistemology that trusts our senses' data as reliable and the mind able to recognize the Truth it conveys. Bravo, Maestro. Finally, in celebration of his teaching about the physical and spiritual senses, one might want to recast John Denver's 'Annie's Song' as an incarnational /mystical hymn a la Balthasar. It might go something like this:

215

You fill up my senses

Like a night in the forest

Like a mountain in springtime

Like a walk in the rain

Like a storm in the desert

Like a sleepy blue ocean

You fill up my senses

Come fill me again

Come let me love you

Let me give my life to you

Let me drown in your laughter

Let me die in your arms

My gracious creator

My spirit's caretaker

You fill up my senses

Come fill me

Again

P.S. Karl Rahner, also a genius, is a bit less optimistic than Balthasar. Rahner confesses and owns his limitations by writing "In the torment of the insufficiencies of everything attainable, we have come to understand that here in this life, all symphonies remain unfinished to which I would say, "If the Shubert fits, wear it," brother Rahner. (c.f. of Schubert's **Unfinished** Symphony)

Part VII

I am Dealt A New Hand

Even People with a purpose have to re-tool or retrain

Happy souls have a purpose, some life interests whether social or personal on which to anchor and structure their journey, and some tune to whistle while they shave or put on make-up as they plan their day. During my twenties, there was a lot to learn, explore, and enjoy while studying abroad. But when I returned to the States, when I finally had my permanent assignment as an assistant priest in St. Pius V in Queens NY, the summit became clouded over in the haze of church politics, particularly over birth control. I stopped reading theology and didn't pick it up again until I joined the faculty of ISEDET, Argentina (1980-3), a center of Liberation Theology. After I returned to the States, I changed focus and enrolled at Rutgers for my MSW, worked two jobs to support my family, and traded my perfect abs for a nice slice of the American pie - wait, make that two slices, waiter, and a Coors, if you please.

Transparency - rare to behold

As a full-time social worker and a part-time Epsicopal priest, (it's a long story) I kept my ministry going but only read enough theology to populate my sermons. Then three years ago, while searching the web for inspiration, I discovered **Bishop Robert Barron**'s YouTube videos which he started producing as a lark in 2006 and then they gained traction. I watched and thought nothing new here, (I had a similar theological background) just a stroll down memory lane I said until I saw his one on Hans Urs Von Balthasar. Game changer!

You might have gotten the impression that I am antagonistic towards Bishop Barron. Totally wrong! I've come neither to bury Caesar nor to praise him. In fact, in his publication "Evangelization Culture," his staff praises the good bishop far better than I could ever hope or want to do. I am a fan of his Sunday sermons and many of his videos and I forward the Spanish version of them to my parishioners as he suggests. But principally, I am indebted to him as a promoter of cultural treasures (with Christian-friendly messages), just as I am indebted to Ed **Sullivan** for introducing me to Edith Piaf, hundreds of Asian plate spinners, and of course, the Beatles who were to me what Bob Dylan still is to Bishop Barron. Now, Ed Sullivan wasn't a performer himself and I view Bishop Barron as more a host and educator than a star. But **that guy Balthasar who he promoted was** unquestionably **a headliner**, a literary master, a guide to the Paschal Mysteries and Trinitarian theology, even more convincing and engaging **at times** than the philosophical tunnels of the Transcendental Thomists from Karl Rahner and the like. Those theologians were engineers and cartologists of subjectivity, truly Olympian thinkers, while Balthasar, their intellectual equal, didn't dig tunnels. He begins by showing the reader the light and the landscape at the end of the tunnel where Jesus resides, 'Jesus – the "Form" and icon of the Father, tangible, welcoming, profiled, and foretold by the OT writers.

Professor Harari Of Israel says all religions are simply stories, myths, and cultural inventions, comfort food. Well, Balthasar's story is one hell of a page-turner and life changer, a better read than Harari's apocalypse speculations which are themselves also works of fiction, until proven otherwise.

Hans Urs Von Balthasar can claim full credit for exposing two major flaws in my spiritual life, first, the lack of a core and central focus for my ministry, and secondly, an irregular and patchy prayer – life that left me riding on empty or settling for a sense of duty instead of gratitude, love and grace in my works of mercy. As I reflect on it, I am reminded of Yeat's poem "The Second Coming" which describes me then, "Turning and Turning in widening gyre. The falcon cannot hear the Falconer. Things fall apart. The Center cannot hold. Mere anarchy is loosed upon the world." (vs the coming together of the tribes (horizons) within us c.f. Isaiah 2:1-5 on Mt Zion) As they say, I was so intent on making outer peace that I neglected inner peace. Balthasar didn't mince words in chastising social gospel advocates like myself when he wrote, "Whoever removes the Cross and its interpretation by the New Testament from the center, in order to replace it, for example, with the social commitment of Jesus to the oppressed as a new center, no longer stands in continuity with the apostolic faith." His writings were a healthy alternative to a steady diet of Liberation Theology and the short-lived Theology of Hope that caused me to think of myself as a savior-on-a-mission, instead of just another voice crying in the desert, a wanderer eating hardtack and sharing his woes with the dunes. I had reduced the REAL SAVIOR to a footnote in my autobiography. It was time, to be honest, to stop going in circles year after year and follow Jesus to the promised land. Thanks to Balthasar, I began to search for and discover the transcendental within the beautiful and, by employing my aesthetic sensitivities, I look for The Divine, both hidden and present in the world and revelation. I was ready to embrace a good Friday just like Dante and Jesus did and to descend to Hades, with Balthasar as my Virgil, to suffer death to ascend born again. I was determined to act on the counsel of **Meister Eckhart,** who wrote, **"When the Soul wants to experience something, she throws out an image in front of her and then steps into it."**

* I was ready to step into the beauty of the cross and leave the unknown god of philosophers to Areopagites while I followed the Crucified. God willing, mine won't be a deathbed conversion. I'd like to pass a little more time as His servant in such a curious world. (Dickinson)

*****

My Foil Bishop Barron takes on Karl Rahner

1) These Roman reflections have been in part - a morality play with two actors: one a bishop, a polyglot a "trata mundo," an apologist, a siren for the disenfranchised Catholic and a prominent spokesperson to many

both inside and out the Catholic Church, etc. He is a theological conservative like his predecessor Bishop Sheen but not as friendly. More a soldier than an ambassador, unfortunately, at a time when the Catholic Church needs all hands on deck and to leave academic Infighting aside (Have I mentioned that Theologians disagree). As I said, I highly recommend Bishop Barron's Sermons and videos, still. I must take exception to his dismissive attitude towards Karl Rahner who was one of the two greatest theologians of the twentieth century by all accounts! Unbelievable! **Bishop Barron claims** in his publication, "Evangelization Culture" Issue #7 pgs. 71-72, that he **read and mastered almost the entire corpus of Rahner in the 1970s and 1980s for his STL and has now moved on.** Does that imply that Rahner is no longer worth reading, Bishop? In the words of the Beatles, "Hey Buffalo Bill, what did you kill, Buffalo Bill?" I admit that when I first read Rahner as a teen, I didn't understand him. He came off as too speculative and cerebral even for me. But when I heard he studied the mystics, I changed gears and read him as a poet and it all made sense. I finally met the saint behind the thinker. For my part, I see no reason in having to choose between a "theology from above" (Balthasar) and a "theology from below." (Rahner) Why not accept both, as Rahner himself has suggested in an interview on YouTube, "It's the CATHOLIC thing to do!" Theologians can disagree, yes, but no one exhausts the mysteries they attempt to explain. As a matter of fact, in an article about mystery published in Karl Rahner's "Theological Investigations" vol. IV, Rahner claims that by their nature, mysteries are inexhaustible, and should be approached humbly Fallible humans shouldn't just walk brazenly up to a burning bush in their everyday sneakers. They should take them off without being asked and tip-toe toward the sacred. On one occasion, you yourself Bishop seemed to have adopted a more **conciliatory** tone when you attended the canonization of John Henry Newman and offered a Q&A On YouTube. There you urged that in the ecumenical dialogue of Anglicans and Roman Catholics, one should focus on common ground issues such as combating secularism, the enemy of them both. That's the spirit, Bishop! Disagree with Rahner all you like as others have but one shouldn't categorically dismiss such a great theologian out of hand. Imagine what a tragic loss it would have been to the world of classical music if aficionados uncritically accepted Tchaikovsky's dismissive evaluation of Brahms' music as being "icing without a cake" and failed to give this conservative master the hearing he deserved.

Discovery

In a recent YouTube (2/12/24) interview Bishop Barron and his guest Fr. Joseph Fessio confessed that both of them were originally planning for a professional baseball career before becoming conservative theologians. In baseball and other sports, you are expected to pick a favorite team to root for. That's an essential part of sporting culture. But the Church is not a competitive sports organization It doesn't celebrate home runs but God-Runs on a scoreboard yet to be revealed. It's the multi-organ **Body of Chris**t. One might prefer the Franciscans over the Jesuits but that's a matter of taste, not substance. I would prefer that we not narrow the playing field to just conservative or liberal theologians but adopt instead the wisdom of Lincoln, "With malice toward none, with charity towards all, with firmness in the right as God gives us to **see the right,** let us finish the work we are in."

Update: Manuel Aside writes in El Pais 6/14/23 that Anton Zeilinger, a Nobel Prize-winning Atomic Physicists Praised Karl Rahner and quoted Rahner's warning i.e. that if the Roman Church doesn't promote Mysticism, the Church itself may end up disappearing. Wow, Bishop Barron, evidently, **some** geniuses are **still reading Rahner!**

Imagine that!

Before announcing the Gotterdammerung of left-leaning theologians I wonder if Bishop Barron knows of the Rahner Society, alive and well at St. John's Seminary, Camarillo?

2) Of course, **the other Robert** is me (with a little "r," whom I trust you know by now as a worker priest with a great future behind me and hopefully a brighter if shorter one ahead. Just a fellow pilgrim ready to share a flagon or a flogging with friends, family, and other pilgrims while we tread the <u>road to Jericho</u>. I have a story too.)

ReTacking my sails

If by chance you as a Roman Catholic were upset (as my mother was) to learn that I even considered transferring my ministry from Rome to Canterbury, trust me, this move was nothing short of traumatic for me as well. Leaving the Roman Church broke my heart. I left over the issue of birth control which my professor Josef Fuchs championed but was overruled. Working in a poor immigrant parish like Pius V, this issue came up constantly and I couldn't in conscience resolve this problem by parroting the **company line**. They still kept asking me, "What does the Church say?" and I was expected to give Paul VI's answer and not Fuch's. When I suggested they just follow their conscience, they nodded and walked away unsatisfied. They were, like me, too Church dependent to risk it. I respected their decision and did the honorable thing on my part and left the ministry. In the interim, I **couldn't bear to attend mass**, it was too painful and distracting to be sitting there envious of the peace around me. I had to tell my priest friend Ken, my buddy from Brooklyn, that I was leaving. He cried. I had to tell my Bishop (who I liked) and he offered to send me to another university for further studies to become a professor (given my potential) but I couldn't in conscience accept his generous offer. He then reluctantly made me an appointment to a clergy review board to state my reasons for leaving and I sadly agreed hoping that my testimony would not upset them or raise doubts about the church in their minds. I felt very protective of their feelings and wished them no harm. I wasn't angry, I was broken, and in need of a job.

In desperation, I decided to pick the brain of an ex-classmate R. Roos who transitioned to the Episcopal church after having been ordained in Rome with me. (He was one of the dirty dozens) I was greatly encouraged listening to his journey, hoping to avoid the pains of hell and panic attacks of dislocation so that maybe one day I too would be **able to continue in the priesthood** and resume pastoral duties. Meanwhile, spiritual healing was my priority. I listened every Sunday to the brilliant sermons of William Sloane Coffin and attended Riverside Church N Y C often as well as Episcopalian Mass at Bill's Institute at St. John the Divine. As I recovered, I decided tentatively and with some hesitation, given the enormity of the step, to seek mentoring and spiritual direction from the Episcopal chaplain of Brooklyn College, Ed Batchelor. I found the authors and text he recommended enlightening and surprisingly clear and well-written. Eventually, I was accepted into the Episcopal Church. I confess I experienced some guilt from the benefits and moments of peace that came from my decision. Evidently, I was still under the neurotic spell of that poem "Patty Blak's Sojourn among the Soupers." My healing process proved to be as arduous as and even longer than my recovery from bypass heart surgery and involved reading a retreat by Anthony de Mello, writings of Sufi mystics, meditation practices, centering prayer, community service (Not court-ordered), and the joy of teaching theology to hopeful seminarians. I finally decided that this new church family was a good fit with its bi-cameral government, ordination of women, championing of social causes, civil and gay rights advocacy, environmental activism, etc. I never will stop loving the church of my youth. I'm cheering from the sidelines with a tip of the hat to Pope Francis, the greatest living pontiff of our times (Sorry, Benedict). If you need further proof of my gratitude and goodwill toward the R. C.

Church, read the poems "Greece" and "Genuflection" by Billy Collins. They can document my journey, my wanderings and discoveries, and my treasured memories.

*If the Past is Prologue

Finally, I am grateful to the **two "secular" conduits** of transcendence in my youth: the **Brooklyn Botanical Gardens and the Brooklyn Museum of Art,** which were Christened by the theologies of Rahner and Von Balthazar respectively fusing priesthood and my social work as complementary roles in my single theo-drama. My training in Rome presaged my future work; <u>from</u> being a student in Rome to becoming a professor in Argentina and New York, <u>from</u> sitting at the bedside of the dying at Santo Spirito hospital in Italy to becoming a hospice social worker, <u>from</u> playing with the kids at the Oratory to becoming a social worker at an adolescent residential school for emotionally handicapped teens and a counselor at Covenant House for runaways. After learning Italian, I added Portuguese and Spanish. I am grateful for my religious training, for scholarships, for my family and my present parish of St. Francis Episcopal Church in Greenville S.C. for my therapy practice, and for Tom, who is my go-to source when my memory fails. ENOUGH. I have to change this cartridge. Ciao! I hope to stay off both **the front and last page** of the news for as long as I can. So, in the words of Umberto who was the greeter at the front door of NAC while we were there and who was a survivor of the Titanic when his ticket was canceled at the last minute, "Bless you."

As a priest

"I have held many things in my hands and lost most of them. BUT whatever I placed in God's hands, THAT I still possess."
(Martin Luther)

Pope Pourri

Life can only be understood backwards but must be lived forward – Soran Kierkgaard

God is present in the moment of choice, not in the order to be seen but in order to be chosen. – C. F. Fuchs.

Sorrow looks back (Pope Paul VI)

Worry looks around (Pope Benedict XVI)

Faith looks up (Pope Francis)

Ralph Waldo Emerson

La commedia e finita

Bibliography

1.   Hans Urs Balthasar, *Engagement with God* (Ignatius Press San Francisco Copyright 1975)

2.   Hans Urs Von Balthasar, *Love Alone Is Credible* (Ignatius Press San Francisco Copyright 2004)

3.   Aidan Nichols, *A KeyTo Balthasar (Baker Academic Publishing Group Grand Rapids, MI Copyright 2011)*

4.   *Angelo Scola, Hans Urs von Balthasar A Theological Style* (William B. Eerdmans Publishing Company Grand Rapids, MI Copyright 1995)

5.   Pope Francis, *Open To God Open To The World* (Bloomsbury Continuum London England Copyright 2018)

6.   Karl Rahner S.J., *The Mystical Way in Everyday Life* (Orbis Book, Maryknoll, N Y Copyright 2010

7.   Stephen Michael DiGiovanni, *Aggiornamento on the Hill of Janus the American College in Rome 1955-1979,* (Midwest Theological Forum Downers Grove, IL Copyright 2016)

8.   Billy Collins, *Questions About Angels* (University of Pittsburgh, PA Copyright 1999)

9.   Ed Gonzalez, *Review: Portrait of Jennie* (Slant Magazine June 27, 2001)

10.   Jonathan Liedl, *Pope Francis calls for "paradigm shift" in theology for the world of today* CNA Vatican City November 1, 2023)

11.   Evangelization of Culture, The Journal of the Word on Fire Institute Issue 7 Spring 2021

Other resources

Michael Sugue, "Gadamer-Hermeneutics and the Human Sciences." YouTube.

Arthur F. Holmes, Gadamer YouTube and the nature of philosophizing.

Bishop Barron, Balthasar, 1 & 2 YouTube.

Jessica Frazier, Gadamer YouTube.

Mark F. Fleischer. St. John's Seminary, Camarillo meeting Karl Rahner Society – June 13, 2015. The soteriology of Karl Rahner and Hans Urs von Balthasar.

Peer Review

November 5, 2022

Robert,

Well, I finally read through your manuscript this weekend. I appreciate your invitation to read it and offer some reflections.

You've had such a vast array of opportunities and rich experiences to study, connect with amazing people, and engage in profound ministry. The focus on your four years in Rome during the late '60's was informative to me, a life-long Episcopalian.

I have had RC colleagues over the years who would periodically allude to the dynamics of their formation in the 1960's, but I'm not aware any of them had the opportunity to study in Rome. One was the pastor of "Blessed Kateri" in Sparta, NJ while I was rector of St. Mary's there. Father Dan was a progressive priest who had been inspired toward his vocation by what he experienced as the fresh air of Vatican II, and then found himself pushing the rock up the mountain during the bulk of his ministry in the 70's, 80's and 90's.

I also had a an Episcopal colleague who occasionally assisted while I was rector of St. Andrew's, Ann Arbor, Charles Witke. Charles had been a professor of classics at U. of Michigan. He periodically made research forays to the Vatican to pour over medieval texts and he'd often come back with wild stories of Vatican intrigue.

I am grateful for your discussions of Gadamer, Rahner, and Balthasar. I've read some of Rahner, but not much of Balthasar or Gadamer. You've inspired me to take a closer look, particularly at Balthasar. I am taken by some of the parallels in his work as you conveyed it with the predominant Eastern Orthodox approach to theological inquiry, which never really divorced theology from prayer. Theology is always mystical theology for the Orthodox -- or, to put it in the terms you reflect, it's always reaching toward the ever-expanding horizon. We can't grasp God it in God's fullness this side of eternity, but we are graced with glimpses through the "transcendentals" which carry the Divine.

A trip to the womb on Gossmerwingo (A Roman Catholic friend)

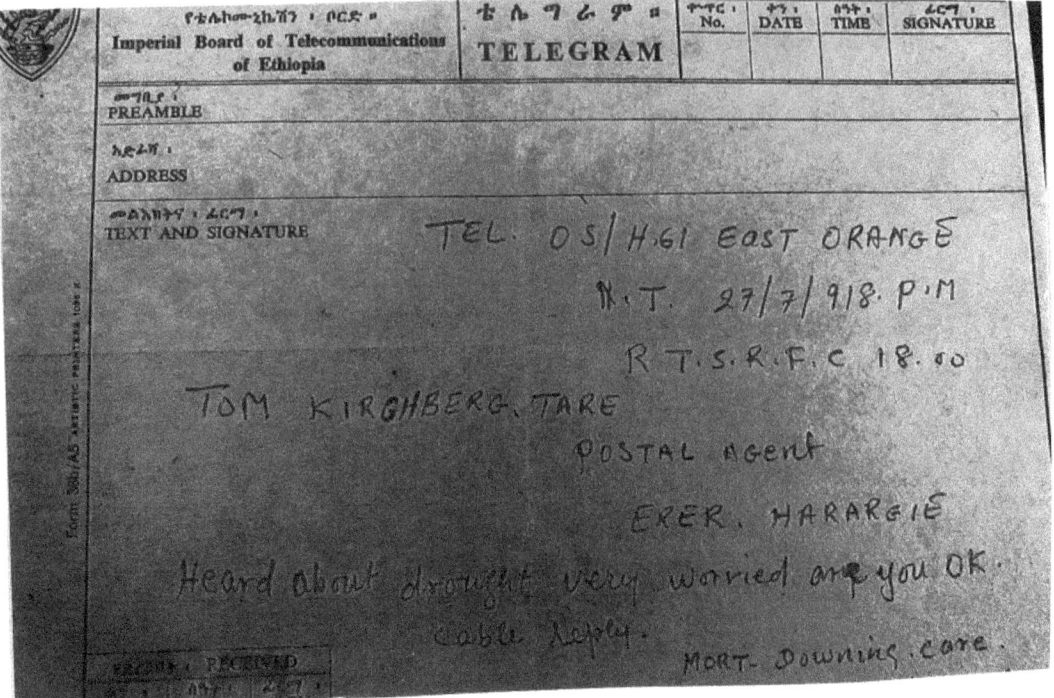

www.ingramcontent.com/pod-product-compliance
Lightning Source LLC
Chambersburg PA
CBHW041112120626
46547CB00019B/2683